Elizabethan
and Jacobean

Elizabethan and Jacobean

BY

F. P. WILSON

OXFORD
AT THE CLARENDON PRESS

Oxford University Press, Ely House, London W. 1

GLASGOW NEW YORK TORONTO MELBOURNE WELLINGTON
CAPE TOWN SALISBURY IBADAN NAIROBI LUSAKA ADDIS ABABA
BOMBAY CALCUTTA MADRAS KARACHI LAHORE DACCA
KUALA LUMPUR SINGAPORE HONG KONG TOKYO

FIRST EDITION 1945
REPRINTED 1946
REPRINTED LITHOGRAPHICALLY IN GREAT BRITAIN
AT THE UNIVERSITY PRESS, OXFORD
BY VIVIAN RIDLER, PRINTER TO THE UNIVERSITY
FROM SHEETS OF THE SECOND IMPRESSION
1952, 1960, 1965, 1969

PREFACE

THESE lectures, the Alexander Lectures in English, were delivered in University College, the University of Toronto, in November 1943. To the University of Toronto, to my audience, and to Principal M. W. Wallace and his colleagues in the Department of English, I am indebted for many kindnesses. Professor W. J. Alexander, in whose honour the lectureship was founded, died in the summer of 1944 in his eighty-ninth year. It is not for one who was in his company for less than a week to add to the tributes already paid to him by his colleagues and pupils, yet to be in his company at all was almost at once to realize something of his greatness as a man and a teacher and to admire that indomitable spirit which kept him young and vigorous in mind to the end. These were the last Alexander lectures that he attended, and I could wish them worthier of his memory.

Since they were delivered, I have added much to the section on poetry, and especially to the section on prose, but without ever thinking of a formal history. I have used, and perhaps abused, the privilege of a lecturer to speak only on those matters that interest him or on which he believes he may usefully express an opinion.

My debts to critics past and present are so many that in a book of this kind I must be allowed to make this one general acknowledgement. To mention all would be (in the old saying) to make my gates bigger than the city. In the notes, however, I mention a few, and I give references to some of the more out-of-the-way quotations.

If a dedicatory leaf were permitted in wartime, I should place on it the words:

TO

HERBERT AND GLADYS DAVIS

with gratitude and affection.

F. P. W.

March, 1945

INTRODUCTORY NOTE

LIKE many a writer who chooses a subject at what seems a comfortable distance from the time of performance, I have often had reason to regret the rashness of my choice. To state or even to suggest some of the main differences between Elizabethan and Jacobean literature in a few hours is a task that might appal a man with more learning and a better gift for generalization than I have. There are two dangers into which it is easy to fall and from which I cannot hope to have escaped. The one is to be tied too narrowly to the literal meaning of the label which I have chosen. The words Elizabethan and Jacobean as I use them in these lectures are only a convenient means of referring to the prevailing modes of the literature written under Elizabeth and under James. They do not imply that Elizabethan literature or Jacobean literature is all of a piece, or that there is any easy common denominator to be found between Hooker and Lyly, Ascham and Nashe on the one hand, or between Jonson and Webster, Donne and Andrewes, Bacon and Burton on the other. And they do not exclude the fact that some Elizabethans continued to write under James much as they had done under Elizabeth. Above all, these labels would be misleading if they implied that the qualities which we recognize as Jacobean rather than Elizabethan are not to be met with before 1603. Epochs of literature do not wait upon the deaths of kings and queens, and it was in the fifteen-nineties, while *The Faerie Queene* was fresh from the press, that the chief modes of Jacobean literature became apparent. In that decade Donne, Jonson, and Bacon first declared themselves, and before the death of the Queen, Shakespeare wrote his *Hamlet*.

The other danger is to exaggerate the break between the Elizabethans and the Jacobeans, to suppose that it was more sudden and more complete than it was. That I may be saved from this danger, I shall begin with a few observations on the continuity of the tradition of learning and the tradition of belief.

I
INHERITANCE

I DO not know that the tradition of learning inherited by both Elizabethans and Jacobeans can be better illustrated than by bringing together for a moment two men who were not much brought together in life, William Cecil, Lord Burghley, and his nephew, Francis Bacon. Cecil, of St. John's College, Cambridge, the brother-in-law of Sir John Cheke, was a good humanist of a sober cast of mind, and like Lord Chesterfield in a later century gave advice to a young man whose character and behaviour suggest that he did not profit from it to the satisfaction of his mentor. In 1578 one of the young undergraduates at King's College was the future translator of *Orlando Furioso* and author of *The Metamorphosis of Ajax*, and it was to John Harington that the elder statesman in that year wrote a letter of advice which sums up the ideal of humanistic education both before Elizabethan and Jacobean times and long after. Endeavour to get understanding, he says in effect. The way to knowledge is not short, and he that undertakes the journey must use good guides.

'For the Latin tongue, Tully chiefly, if not only; for the Roman story (which is exceeding fit for a Gentleman to understand) Livy and Caesar; for Logic and Philosophy, Aristotle and Plato. And so, in all tongues and sciences the most notable and approved (as your tutor can best tell you) not dealing with over great variety of books, which young men delight in; and yet, in mine opinion, they breed but a scattering of the mind. For as Seneca saith, "*Cauta lectio prodest, varia delectat.*" . . . Sit not in your study reading, when you should be in the hall hearing. . . . You shall reach more discerning of truth in an hour's reasoning with others, than a week's writing by yourself; though I know nothing I would have you more use than writing. . . . In writing, to seek variety of invention, to make choice of words and phrases, to use apt examples, and good imitation, I know to be very good things; but if you follow the trade of Sir John Cheke (who was one of the sweetest flowers that hath comen in my time out of the garden you grow in) you cannot do better. One manner of his, amongst divers excellent, was this, to appoint those that were under him, and that he desired should most profit, to take a piece of Tully, and to translate it into English, and after, laying their books aside, to translate the same again into Latin, and then to compare them with the book, and to consider which were done aptly, or unproperly; and how near Tully's phrase was followed in the Latin, and the most sweet and sensible writing in English; continuing with this kind of exercise once or twice in a week, for two or three years, you shall come to write (as he did) singularly in both tongues, which is most necessary and most commendable.

'Last of all, whether you speak or write or whatsoever you do, I would advise you to remember Cicero his lesson, which is good in learning but better in living: "*Omnis actio vacare debet temeritate et negligentia.*" Thus first fearing and praising God, and following your book and good company, you shall become a great comfort to your father, and praise to your master; an honour to the University that breeds you; a fit servant for the Queen and your country, for which you were born, and to which, next God, you are most bound; a good stay to yourself; and no small joy to your friends.'

Education by grammatical exegesis of the greatest works in the arts and the sciences, of 'the best that is known and thought in the world', the training of the judgement through logic, such study of rhetoric as will lead a man not only to the writing of good Latin but to 'the most sweet and sensible writing in English', the aim to produce a Christian orator who shall put his learning and wisdom at the service of the state, these are ideals which had never entirely perished since Cicero's *doctus orator* had become the Chris-

tian orator of St. Augustine. Nor is it an ideal which
Francis Bacon would have disputed. To him too the
dominion over nature which man had lost by his fall was
only to be repaired by arts and sciences applied to the uses
of human life; and it was to be repaired not by dialectic
speculation but by methods which differ from those of
traditional grammar only in their insistence that to the
knowledge of man and nature inherited from past ages in
books must be added a more diligent inquiry into the ways
of man and nature as they may be investigated in the
laboratory of life. Bacon was neither an 'ancient' nor a
'modern', but one who desired to establish a 'sociable
intercourse' between antiquity and 'proficience'. An eloquent passage in praise of the tradition of learning is to
be found in one of those places where Bacon is using
eloquence, as Cicero and St. Augustine had used it, to
sway the mind to truth and stir the will to right action, one
of those passages which by the dignity of the language and
beauty of the cadence and imagery led Shelley to exclaim
that Bacon was a poet.

'Leaving the vulgar arguments, that by learning man
excelleth man in that wherein man excelleth beasts; that by
learning man ascendeth to the heavens and their motions,
where in body he cannot come; and the like; let us conclude
with the dignity and excellency of knowledge and learning in
that whereunto man's nature doth most aspire; which is immortality or continuance; for to this tendeth generation, and
raising of houses and families; to this buildings, foundations,
and monuments; to this tendeth the desire of memory, fame,
and celebration; and in effect, the strength of all other human
desires. We see then how far the monuments of wit and learning are more durable than the monuments of power or of the
hands. For have not the verses of Homer continued twenty-
five hundred years or more, without the loss of a syllable or
letter; during which time infinite palaces, temples, castles,

cities, have been decayed and demolished? It is not possible to have the true pictures or statues of Cyrus, Alexander, Caesar, no nor of the kings or great personages of much later years; for the originals cannot last, and the copies cannot but leese of the life and truth. But the images of men's wits and knowledges remain in books, exempted from the wrong of time and capable of perpetual renovation. Neither are they fitly to be called images, because they generate still, and cast their seeds in the minds of others, provoking and causing infinite actions and opinions in succeeding ages. So that if the invention of the ship was thought so noble, which carrieth riches and commodities from place to place, and consociateth the most remote regions in participation of their fruits, how much more are letters to be magnified, which as ships pass through the vast seas of time, and make ages so distant to participate of the wisdom, illuminations, and inventions, the one of the other?'

The vitality of this tradition of learning might be illustrated from the Elizabethan Hooker and from the sermons of the Jacobean Andrewes or Donne, and some notion of its persistence within a century may be gathered from the extent to which Henry Peacham in his *Complete Gentleman* of 1622 cared to borrow from Sir Thomas Elyot's *The Governor* of 1531; but humble examples from the lay sermons of the Elizabethan pamphleteer Nashe and the Jacobean pamphleteer Dekker show it operating over the centuries. Nashe who had studied the *trivium* and the *quadrivium* (however dilatorily) at that great seat of learning and of patristic study, St. John's College, Cambridge, had no need of a florilegium in which to read the Fathers, though he probably used one. 'Turn over the ancient Fathers, and mark how sweet and honeysome they are in the mouth, and how musical and melodious in the ear. No Orator was ever more pleasingly persuasive than humble Saint Augustine.' Nashe's disciple, Thomas Dekker, not a university wit and one who had never travelled far from the music of Bow Bells, took his knowledge of the Fathers from the *Flores Doctorum* of Thomas Hibernicus, a thirteenth-century Irishman whose anthology, copied and reprinted over centuries, introduced thousands to the eloquence and wisdom of the Fathers and of the classical moralists. This eloquence and this wisdom permeate the lay sermons of this popular pamphleteer. When he writes of the heavenly City—'There is security without fear; peace without invasion; wealth without diminishing; honours without envy; there is all blessedness, all sweetness, all life, all eternity'—the rhetorical pattern and the sentiments go back to the Fathers: 'Ibi est lux sine defectu, gaudium sine gemitu, . . . vita sine morte; . . . ubi dignitas, ubi sanctitas, ubi vita, ubi aeternitas.' As with Nashe so with Dekker, the very cast of his sentences bears witness to the durability of that *translatio studii* which passes from Cicero to St. Augustine, which lives on in Bede and Alcuin, which survives the supremacy of dialectics in the later Middle Ages, and is restored to abundant life by Petrarch and by Erasmus and other humanists of the fifteenth and sixteenth centuries.

As in the tradition of learning, so in the tradition of belief, there is no break between Elizabethan and Jacobean. The dramatists, alike with the poets and prose-writers, assumed a Christian universe. Their plays are worked out for the most part in terms of this world, but the beliefs and moral values of the Christian religion are not challenged. This was not merely a matter of censorship; it was a matter of acceptance even if with some writers acceptance ended with lip-service. Of the two famous writers who earned a reputation for atheism among some of their contemporaries, Raleigh and Marlowe, the one wrote a History of the World which left its mark on *Paradise Lost* and was accepted by the Puritans as a text-book illustrating and justifying the ways of God to men; the other wrote the one important play of that age which is explicitly Christian and religious in plot, a kind of morality play in which a man's good angel and his bad angel are presented on the stage to contest for the possession of his soul, a play in which the pride of the flesh and the pride of knowledge are indeed powerfully presented, in spite of a mangled text and much triviality, but one in which these are emphatically brought to confusion and the orthodox doctrines of redemption and damnation announced with a power not approached in English drama before or since. If then a Jacobean tragedy ends without reference to the joys of heaven or the terrors of hell, it is not because the dramatists disbelieved in an after-life for the virtuous and for the wicked. It was a church-going and sermon-reading age, one in which reflections upon the ultimate issues of life and death were encouraged not merely by preachers and moralists but by popular pamphleteers and ballad-writers, and this seriousness impregnates the drama even when it seems to a superficial view predominantly secular. To disbelieve in that age would indeed have brought chaos not only to the individual man but to the universe in which he lived. The age believed, as the tenth Homily puts it, that 'Almighty God hath created and appointed all things in heaven, earth and waters in a most excellent and perfect order', a belief which forms the *point de repère* of Shakespeare's history plays and is given its finest expression in the famous speech of Ulysses on 'degree' in *Troilus and Cressida*. They believed in a Chain of Being with exquisitely delicate gradations from God and the angels down to vegetables and minerals, a chain with no missing link, for *Natura non facit saltus*—'Thy creatures leap not' as George Herbert says. They believed in man as the microcosm or little world of the universe, placed in a position between angels and beasts and partaking in his own nature both of God and of the lower creation.

> God first made angels bodiless, pure minds,
>> Then other things, which mindless bodies be;
> Last, He made Man, th' horizon 'twixt both kinds,
>> In whom we do the World's abridgement see.

They believed that by the Fall reason was overwhelmed and knowledge darkened, but that man could be saved by supernatural law as revealed in the Scriptures. And many of them believed also in the law of nature: that at the Fall the soul did not become a *tabula rasa*, but preserved some traces of its past glory. No longer able to inform itself of the nature of things by descent from the universal to particulars as was Adam when he gave all creatures names according to their natures, it might yet frame general and universal notions by induction from particulars, know its natural immortality by discourse of reason, and by the heavenly gift of eloquence persuade others to all good order. Such beliefs, together with the belief in the four elements and the four humours, they inherited with little or no modification from the Middle Ages, and the stability of the system, slowly built up over the centuries by the speculations of Jews and Gentiles, Christians and pagans alike, was not seriously threatened in Elizabethan or Jacobean times. True, there was the Copernican system. True, an Englishman, Thomas Digges, had in 1576 accepted this system and gone on to maintain that the universe was infinite and the stars numberless, that they are located at varying distances from the centre, the sun, and extend through infinite space. We may not indeed suppose that the astronomical speculation of the day had as little effect on contemporary minds as Einstein's revision of the Newtonian universe has had on the minds of those of us who are not mathematicians and physicists; for one thing, modern science is unintelligible to all but specialists, and for another, there is nothing in the modern case that is comparable to the belief in the correspondences between the macrocosm and the microcosm—the four elements and the four humours, the seven planets and the seven ages of man, &c.—or to the belief in the literal inspiration of the Bible. But when we remember that other astronomies had seemed successfully to patch up the Ptolemaic system, and that the day had not yet come when Revelation had always to be compatible with natural Reason—for, as Bacon said, we must believe, even if Reason is reluctant, for Divinity is founded only upon the word and oracle of God, and not upon the light of nature—we may doubt whether even Donne or Milton, much less any Elizabethan dramatist, spent a sleepless night over the attempts of astronomers to 'salve all appearances'.

Donne's intellectual curiosity in scientific speculation provides him with convenient illustrations in the *First Anniversary* of the decay of nature and the disorder of the world and in the *Second Anniversary* of the soul's ignorance in this life, but in both poems he is applying modern instances to support a medieval *De Contemptu Mundi*, and he had certainly not been driven to this view by the speculations of a Copernicus or a Tycho Brahe. Robert Burton, according to Wood an exact mathematician, may have been better seen in scientific speculation than Donne. His interest is shown both by the books in his library and by the use ·which he made of them, notably in the 'digression of the air' in the second Partition of *The Anatomy of Melancholy*. The logic of the structure of his book had brought him to the point where he was to consider the effect of air and climate upon the constitution, and with some relief he relaxes from the close work of dissection and roams at will in the exciting air of speculation. More amusing passages may be found in the section on love melancholy, more eloquent and moving in the section on religious melancholy, but none gives a better idea of the alertness of this secluded scholar—who had never travelled 'but in map or card'—to any motion of the human mind. Men like Barlowe or Hakewill flatly opposed the theories of Copernicus as contrary to scripture, reason, and sense; but Burton's attitude is one of excited and amused scepticism. Astronomers with their eccentrics and epicycles seemed to him like tinkers who stop one hole and make two, and between them the world was tossed in a blanket: 'they hoise the earth up and down like a ball, make it stand and go at their pleasures'. Burton is content to say of these matters—as of what happens to cuckoos and swallows in the winter-time—'as yet we know not'. There is no 'irritable reaching after fact', any more than there is in *Paradise Lost*. In Burton, the new takes its place beside the old in a rich world of speculation. ''Tis an even lay', but faith is not assailed, and the universe in which he breathes is still in many ways medieval.

He tells the story of a hermit tempted by the devil in the habit of a young market wench; as the hermit was on the point of forgetting his vows 'she vanished on a sudden, and the Devils in the air laughed him to scorn'. 'Whether this be a true story, or a tale', he adds, 'I will not much contend: it serves to illustrate this which I have said'. An older writer might not have questioned the truth of the story, but he would have made the same analogical use of it. This mixture of scepticism and belief may be noticed in the use of the simile from natural history, a kind of imagery prevalent in patristic literature and very popular in the sixteenth century. One of the reasons why there had been no strict examination of the 'irregulars of nature', with due rejection of fables and popular errors, writes Bacon in *The Advancement of Learning* (1605), was 'the use of the opinion in similitudes and ornaments of speech'. In the very 'modern' *Aphorisms Civil and Military* (1613) of Robert Dallington, the maxims of which are based upon the history of the sceptical and cynical Guicciardini as Machiavelli's were based on Livy, analogy after analogy is drawn from fabulous natural history—from the panther that entices its victims by the sweetness of its breath and hides its ugly face lest it frighten them away, to the Ethiopian yale with two horns which it can move forward in offence or backward in defence or the one forward and the other backward to both uses at once. It would be a strange conclusion, writes Bacon—again in *The Advancement*—'if a man should use a similitude for ornament or illustration sake, borrowed from nature or history according to vulgar conceit, as of a basilisk, an unicorn, . . . that therefore he must needs be thought to affirm the matter thereof positively to be true', but it was at least possible for a man willingly to suspend disbelief. The time was at hand—but it had not arrived—when the old similes, if they survived at all, survived as dead metaphors, and men talked about licking a thing into shape in ignorance of the maternal habits of the bear. Similarly the old astronomies and the new were available to Donne and to Milton for their poetical or homiletical purposes. By the time of Eachard, however, the 'reign of Atoms' had succeeded the days of '*Materia Prima* and Occult Qualities', and in his *Grounds and Occasions of the Contempt of the Clergy and Religion* (1670) he gives the ironical advice to the preacher: 'He that has got a set of similitudes calculated according to the old philosophy, and Ptolemy's system of the world, must burn his commonplace book, and go a gleaning for new ones.'

Perhaps we may take Sir Walter Raleigh as in himself an epitome of the eclecticism of the most cultured spirits of the age. The obscurity especially of Raleigh's private life dissuaded Gibbon from making him the subject of an elaborate biography, but a free-thinking 'philosopher' like Gibbon might well have been deterred by the seeming contradictions of Raleigh's beliefs. Now we find him despising the vanity of human effort, 'the false and dureless pleasures of this stage-play world', and now eager to be a man of action, once more to recover fame, riches, glory, and 'reputation lost'. We find this so-called atheist proclaiming that in the glorious lights of heaven we perceive a shadow of God's divine countenance; 'in his merciful provision for all that live, his manifold goodness; and lastly, in creating and making existent the world universal by the absolute art of his own word, his power and almightiness'. And we find this man of science with an enthusiasm for experiment believing also in the decay of nature and the approaching dissolution of the world: 'and as the Devil our most industrious enemy was ever most diligent: so is he now more laborious than ever: the long day of mankind drawing fast towards an evening, and the world's tragedy and time near at an end'. Many have been baffled by the contrarieties found in the men of this age and have felt that they exceeded the measure of inconsistency to be allowed to human nature in all ages; but the inconsistency is more apparent to ages that had ceased to believe in the direct intervention of God and the Devil in human affairs and had exchanged a divine universe for a mechanical.

The dramatists were not much interested, as dramatists, in dogma or a philosophical synthesis, but they were interested in the law of nature, in the problem of evil and suffering, in the life of action and the life of contemplation, in the pull of this world and how far it can be reconciled with man's aspirations for the next, in mutability, and some of them were especially interested in man's behaviour at what many felt to be the supreme moment of life—at death.

While their plays are concerned with men and women and their ways upon earth, this background of a Christian universe under divine ordinance is assumed and is present in allusions the full force of which escape a reader unfamiliar with their world. The enormity of Faustus's wish in the agony of his last moments

> Stand still, you ever-moving spheres of heaven,
> That time may cease, and midnight never come

was felt more forcibly by men who believed with Hooker:

'Let any principal thing, as the sun, the moon, any one of the heavens or elements, but once cease or fail, or swerve, and who doth not easily conceive that the sequel thereof would be ruin both to itself and whatsoever dependeth on it?'

And the falsity of his boastful cry

> This word 'damnation' terrifies not me,
> For I confound hell in Elysium

would strike home to an audience well aware of the difference between the Elysium of 'the old philosophers' and the terrors of a Christian hell. This age, then, was not an age wandering between two worlds 'one dead, the other powerless to be born', for the old world was very far from being dead, and while the shape of things to come was beginning to be discernible in Jacobean times, the dramatists, if we discount the work of those who had no serious reflections to make upon God, man, or society, were conservatives almost to a man. The most obvious exceptions were Marlowe and Chapman, if we exclude Ford as belonging to a later age. Perhaps we should not be so tempted to find in Marlowe's plays the evidence for a kind of Elizabethan Shelley advocating the necessity of atheism but for the testimonies of Thomas Kyd and other informers; and while Chapman's beliefs may not be summed up in a phrase—for they were as peculiar to himself as Milton's—it may be said that there was a strong infusion of Christianity in his blend of stoicism and neo-platonism.

Tidy and settled as their universe may seem to us, there was room enough for wide-reaching speculation upon the nature and destiny of man. As with us, so with them, much if not most of this speculation was inherited from past ages. Is the world arbitrarily and inexplicably controlled by Fortune? Or is it, like the next, controlled not by 'the blind wheel of Fortune' but by God? Is man the sport of the stars or Fortune or has he a judging wit and choosing will? Does God reward the virtuous and punish the sinful now as well as hereafter? Or should we believe that we do not know why in this world God sometimes suffers the bad man to have joy and the good man sorrow, the wicked to live sound and the godly to lie bedrid, but must accept these facts as proofs of God's inscrutable judgements and unsearchable ways? 'Man is like to vanity:' says the Psalmist, 'his days are as a shadow that passeth away'; and yet if we consider man in general, as he is mortal, and without reference to the life eternal, what apprehension has his spirit and how large is his capacity! Again, what strange combination is that of a nature incorporeal and a nature corporeal by which the whole becomes a living creature, 'a work so admirable, that it is able to amaze the mind!' And if we consider the world in which man lives, who is able to recount the beauty and use of the creatures which God has set before his eyes?

'The universal gracefulness of the heavens, the earth, and the sea, the brightness of the light in the Sun, Moon, and Stars, the shades of the woods, the colours and smells of flowers, the numbers of birds and their varied hues and songs, the many forms of beasts and fishes, whereof the least are the rarest . . . and the strange alterations in the colour of the sea, . . . the day's reciprocation with the night, the temperateness of the air, and the works of nature in the barks of trees and skins of beasts.'

I am quoting from Healey's translation of *The City of God* dedicated to William Herbert, Earl of Pembroke, in 1610 by the man who had published Shakespeare's Sonnets a year before. These great commonplaces of the mystery of soul and body, of man's destiny on earth, of life and death, are all to be found in St. Augustine.

II

THE ELIZABETHANS AND THE
JACOBEANS

SO far I have been insisting on the many links which bound both Elizabethans and Jacobeans to their past, and I have done so in order to escape the error of exaggerating the differences between the two generations as these are to be noticed in their literature. For there are differences; to maintain that there is no change would be as gross an error as to maintain that all is change. The simplest attempt to state the change—so simple that it cannot be true—would be to contrast the optimism of the Elizabethans with the pessimism of the Jacobeans, adding references to the gaiety of the Court of Elizabeth and the corrupt humours of the Court of James. Contemporary authors can easily be cited. Drayton dedicates his poems of 1627 to those gentlemen 'who in these declining times have yet in your brave bosoms the sparks of that sprightly fire of your courageous ancestors, and to this hour retain the seeds of their magnanimity and greatness', and near the end of James's reign John Chamberlain pointedly calls the 17th of November, the anniversary of Elizabeth's accession, 'the happiest day that ever England had to my remembrance'. Both men of course were old Elizabethans, as were John Harington, Daniel, and George Chapman, but other statements of the kind could be collected from younger men to whom Elizabeth was only a childhood's memory. The debate on this point continues, but I am not sure that it is profitable. The Court of Elizabeth did not seem gay to Raleigh or to the author of *Mother Hubberd's Tale*, and it was Spenser's patron, Sidney, not a Jacobean, who wrote these lines with their splendid epiphonematical close:

> O sweet woods, the delight of solitariness!
> O how much I do like your solitariness!
> Here nor treason is hid, veiled in innocence,
> Nor envy's snaky eye finds any harbour here;
> Nor flatterers' venomous insinuations,
> Nor cunning humorists' puddled opinions,
> Nor courteous ruin of proffered usury,
> Nor time prattled away, cradle of ignorance,
> Nor causeless duty, nor cumber of arrogance,
> Nor trifling title of vanity dazzleth us,
> Nor golden manacles stand for a paradise.
> Here wrong's name is unheard, slander a monster is.
> Keep thy sprite from abuse; here no abuse doth haunt.
> What man grafts in a tree dissimulation?

And on the other hand Bacon observed in James's reign, not Elizabeth's, that although the world was in the autumn of its days, to that autumn was appointed the bearing and fructifying of the plant of knowledge. Perhaps the insistence on Jacobean 'pessimism' is due to a too exclusive attention to Jacobean tragedy and the poetry of Donne. Burton was as much concerned with the pathology of the human mind as Tourneur or Webster, yet in a book which of all books might be expected to assume the universal decay of nature he observed that 'Nature is not so effete . . . or so lavish to bestow all her gifts upon an age, but hath reserved some for posterity, to shew her power that she is still the same, and not old and consumed'. Both ages indeed were so receptive that it is impossible to sum up their moods in a phrase. The welter of information which Burton jostles together in his *Anatomy* is characteristic of an age that was eclectic rather than critical, was better pleased to absorb than to reject. I will not deny that there were pessimists among the Jacobeans, that is, men without hope for this world if not for the next, but this is hardly a distinguishing mark between the two ages. What would have been new and shocking to both ages would have been a belief in perfectibility.

As the sixteenth century grew older the works of more and more speculative writers became better known in England, and speculation was exercised more freely, and with more and more emphasis on man's life in this world. 'Traffic and travel', writes John Lyly, 'hath woven the nature of all nations into ours, and made this land like arras, full of device, which was broad-cloth, full of workmanship.' He is thinking in part of the growing luxury of the time, or as some would put it of the rising standard of living, and of the importation of foreign fashions in dress and manners, and shaking his head over them, though not so vigorously as Roger Ascham in *The Schoolmaster* and William Harrison in his *Description of England*. Travel was nothing new, and perhaps no Elizabethan woman had travelled so far afield as did the Wife of Bath in fiction and Margery Kempe in fact; but what was new was the traffic and distribution of ideas by means of the printing-press and the bombardment of England with ideas ancient, medieval, and modern which grew in volume as the sixteenth century became older and (presumably) the reading public increased. By the end of King James's reign there were few of the great classics of Rome, Italy, and Spain which could not be read in English, while those who could read them in the originals were more and more being supplied with English editions. That the ancient moralists and historians —not only Seneca, Tacitus, Livy, Suetonius, but also Plutarch—were so made available is well known, for the Elizabethans and Jacobeans never wrote better prose than in their translations of the classics; but also available in English were many modern writers who, while basing their works upon the classics, transformed the teaching of the past by their own genius and by the very fact that they were applying it to the conditions of a new age.

Readers whose knowledge of Elizabethan and Jacobean literature is confined to anthologies of poetry—the sonnet, the erotic poem, the pastoral, the secular lyric—may be surprised at the statement that the main preoccupations of Elizabethans and Jacobeans alike were with religion, theological controversy, and what may be called compendiously if loosely moral philosophy, yet it was so. What distinguishes the Jacobean age from the Elizabethan is its more exact, more searching, more detailed inquiry into moral and political questions and its interest in the analysis of the mysteries and perturbations of the human mind. Next to the moralists of the Silver Age—and especially Seneca, Tacitus, and Plutarch—the writers whose works were most congenial to the new age were men like Machiavelli, Francesco Guicciardini, Bodin, Huarte, Cardan, Lipsius, Montaigne, Charron, all Catholics with the exception (for a time) of Bodin and Lipsius, most of them writers who claimed for man an intellectual and moral liberty which made them suspect to the orthodox Christianity of a later generation and sometimes of their own, writers intimately acquainted with the wisdom of the classical moralists and disconcertingly and sometimes unwittingly confusing the boundaries between Christian wisdom and natural wisdom, writers condemned by believers or welcomed by 'libertins' as sceptics, naturalists, or rationalists. Works by all these men had been translated into English by 1625, but translation is only partial evidence of the extent to which they were being read by Englishmen. With the exception of Machiavelli, whose maxims were attacked within the sixteenth century both by the Reformation and the Counter-Reformation, their writings were hardly questioned by their English admirers, who transformed what they took from these moderns, giving to it their own native moral twist, as much as these in turn had transformed the teachings of the classical moralists.

Of these writers the greatest and in their effect upon English thought the most important were Machiavelli and Montaigne. Not much of the essential Machiavelli appeared in the English translations of *The Art of War* (1560–2) and the *Florentine History* (1595), and in 1560 'this worthy Florentine and Italian' could be recommended without reserve to the Queen and to 'all good English hearts, most lovingly and friendly to be entertained, embraced and cherished'. But some Elizabethans knew more of the real Machiavelli than they could gather from these translations or from the caricatures of the man and his doctrine played upon their stage. While translations of the *Discourses* and *The Prince* were not printed (presumably were not allowed to be printed) before 1636 and 1640, the originals could be read in editions printed at London in 1584. By no Englishman before Fulke Greville and Bacon was the Machiavellism of Machiavelli more fully absorbed than by Gabriel Harvey. *The Prince* was worth more to him than the *Institutio Principis Christiani* of Erasmus, and in the margins of his books the Cambridge scholar did not conceal his admiration for one that was 'not to seek how to use the wicked world, the flesh, and the devil'. But Harvey wisely kept his opinions to himself. One of the earliest defences of Machiavelli to appear in an English book is in William Jones's translation (1594) of Lipsius's *Six Books of Politics*. Lipsius is about to distinguish between light deceit (*fraus levis*) which he recommends, middle deceit (*fraus media*) which he tolerates, and great deceit (*fraus magna*) which he condemns; and after quoting Plutarch's Lysander to the effect that he who cannot prevail by the lion's skin must put on the fox's, and Pindar's praise of him who in battle has the courage of a lion and in counsel the craftiness of the fox, he observes that the man who is not ignorant of those things that happen in this life will agree with St. Basil that there exists a kind of deceit that is honest and laudable; such a man will not 'so strictly condemn the Italian fault-writer (who poor soul is laid at of all hands)'. The marginal comment is also englished by Jones: 'Some kinds of persons rage too much against Machiavell.'

Like Machiavelli, Montaigne looked into the moralists and historians of old and found their findings consonant with his own; but whereas Machiavelli is a doctrinaire who codifies human conduct, establishes fixed lines of advance and retreat in that country where Fortune permits man to be master of his fate, cuts into the corruption of human nature with the precision and something of the detachment of the surgeon using his scalpel, Montaigne establishes no system unless it be the free and disinterested inquiry into the vagaries of the human mind, and especially of his own. Questions of practical morality absorb them both, but Machiavelli in so far as they concern man in society, Montaigne much more as they concern man in the presence of himself. Like the Jacobeans, however, Montaigne accepts the Christian faith and the dogmas of his Church, and indeed the effect of his examination is to inspire the question what would happen to man without a supervenient act of grace:

'Let us now but consider man alone without other help, armed but with his own weapons, and unprovided of the grace and knowledge of God, which is all his honour, all his strength, and all the ground of his being. Let us see what hold-fast or free-hold he hath in this gorgeous and goodly equipage. Let him with the utmost power of his discourse make me understand upon what foundation he hath built those great advantages and odds he supposeth to have over other creatures. Who hath persuaded him that this admirable moving of heaven's vaults, that the eternal light of these lamps so fiercely rolling over his head, that the horror-moving and continual motion of this infinite vast ocean, were established and continue so many ages for his commodity and service? Is it possible to imagine anything so ridiculous as this miserable and wretched creature, which is not so much as master of himself, exposed and subject to offences of all things, and yet dareth call himself Master and Emperor of this Universe? In whose power it is not to know the least part of it, much less to command the same. And the privilege, which he so fondly challengeth, to be the only absolute creature in this huge world's frame, perfectly able to know the absolute beauty and several parts thereof, and that he is only of power to yield the great Architect thereof due thanks for it, and to keep account both of the receipts and layings out of the world. Who hath sealed him this patent? Let him shew us his letters of privilege for so noble and so great a charge. Have they been granted only in favour of the wise? Then concern they but a few. Are the foolish and wicked worthy of so extraordinary a favour? Who being the worst part of the world, should they be preferred before the rest?'

The passage comes in Montaigne's longest essay, 'The Apology for Raymond Sebond', and some critics have suspected Montaigne of irony in that he should choose to defend Sebond's claims for the law of nature, excessive to the point of unorthodoxy, by an equally unorthodox abrogation of the law of nature. Others see in his essay no irony and no expression of faith, but a typical Renaissance development of a paradox: a return to a work which he had translated in his youth at the command of his father for the intellectual interest of seeing how *pro* may be answered with *contra*. But the accusation that the breach which Montaigne makes between faith and reason was a covert plea for rationalism appears to be unjust, and Montaigne is not to blame for the use made of his method by the 'libertins' of a later generation. The fideism of 'The Apology' is, however, but an intermediate stage between the *stoïcisme de tête* of the earliest essays and the epicureanism of the latest, and while the essayist always keeps an orthodox catholicism in reserve the interest is in threading the labyrinth of the mind, sensibility, and senses of man, the whole personality of the natural man. It is as much upon the analysis of himself as upon the rational morality of the ancients or his observation of the moderns that Montaigne bases his conclusion that man is *divers et ondoyant*, 'a wonderful, vain, divers, and wavering subject' in Florio's translation, 'it is very hard to ground any directly-constant and uniform judgement upon him'.

Before Florio's translation got into print, three Englishmen had borrowed Montaigne's title—Bacon in 1597, Cornwallis in 1600, Robert Johnson in 1601—and had published books of Essays. Bacon's Essays are not works of supererogation; they are as much a part of the *Instauratio Magna* as the *Silva Silvarum*. When in *The Advancement of Learning* and in the *De Augmentis Scientiarum* Bacon turns to survey those parts of learning which lie 'fresh and waste' he gives much more space to Human Philosophy, the knowledge of ourselves segregate or conjugate, than to Natural Philosophy. The Essays are part of his programme for the practical examination of the causes of human conduct, and he profits from his knowledge of Machiavelli on man conjugate and Montaigne on man segregate. Something like the Essay was known to Seneca and Plutarch, as Bacon observed and as Montaigne had in mind when he praised Plutarch's 'little works' and Seneca's Epistles as 'the best and most profitable part of their writings', yet in a new age it takes on new forms. So the 'character', which emerges about the same time, owes much to Theophrastus, yet becomes something new. Its function was to say what men are and to say it with brevity, with wit, and with paradox; and the extraordinary popularity of the character after its form had been devised by Lodge, Jonson, Hall, Overbury, and others, is evidence of the fascination which the minute analysis of moral or social types had for the seventeenth century. About the turn of the century historical writing, too, takes on a new form. More and more the chroniclers are attacked for their indiscriminate recording of events, and historians like Sir John Hayward begin to insist on 'Order, Poise [i.e. weight], and Truth' as the requisites of a just history, and on 'knowledge, judgement, and sincerity' as the qualities of a good historian. Bacon praises Machiavelli and others for writing what men do and not what they ought to do, and he saw to it that his own essays came home to 'men's business and bosoms'. Of the three faculties into which he divided the rational soul, Memory, Imagination, and Reason, the second, it is becoming clear, has nothing to offer the moral essayist or the historian. In 1618 Hayward is attacking those historians of their own country who make things 'seem not as they are, but as they would have them, no otherwise almost than Comedies and Tragedies are fashioned by their Authors', and memory or documentary evidence triumphs over imagination or 'the most senseless fictions' of Geoffrey of Monmouth with his legends of the Trojan ancestry of the ancient Britons.

It is not merely in the prose that a change manifests itself. The change may be suggested by reference to Cornwallis's praise of Montaigne's desire to know Brutus's private actions—what he did in his tent rather than in battle; to Bacon pleading for a patient inquiry into the secrets not only of nature but of human nature; to Burton exploring the hearts of men and finding windmills in one man's and a hornet's nest in another's. But the change may also be suggested by reference to Donne probing the inner recesses of his mind in secular and religious lyric with the heat of passion and the light of reason; to Jonson anatomizing the humours of men and the deformity of the times with constant courage and contempt of fear; and to Shakespeare passing from the tragedies of fate in a *Richard III* or a *Romeo and Juliet* to the tormented and divided soul of a Hamlet or a Macbeth. Parallels between literature and other arts are dangerous and usually delusory, but if, as some hold, the essential difference between baroque art and the art of the High Renaissance lies in the attempt to express and enhance elapsing moments of ever-changing Nature rather than the idea of Nature as a perennial reality, then Donne's poetry has a better claim to be called baroque than Spenser's, Webster's plays than Marlowe's, and Bacon's prose than Ascham's or Hooker's. To the new age, so often sceptical, tentative, and self-conscious in its exploration of hidden motives, a new style was necessary, a style that could express the mind as it was in movement, could record the thought at the moment it arose in the mind. The amplifications and formal figures of Elizabethan rhetoric were as unsuitable for their purposes as the roundness of the Ciceronian period wheeling its way to a long foreseen conclusion. The new style appears in the fifteen-nineties in the poetry of Chapman, Donne, Raleigh, and others, in the prose of Bacon, in the plays of Shakespeare and Jonson. It is the style of 'So, so, break off this last lamenting kiss', of 'Cover her face; mine eyes dazzle; she died young'. A loosening of rhythm, a closer approximation to the diction of common life that is not incompatible with magnificence, a rejection of copiousness and elaborate word-schemes— these make possible the concentration of Donne's love poems and of Bacon's prose, and the tragic vision of Shakespeare, Webster, and Middleton.

III

PROSE

WHEN in *The Advancement of Learning* Bacon looks back to English prose in the time of Ascham, he sees it as a period when men hunted more after words than matter, 'more after the choiceness of the phrase, and the round and clean composition of the sentence, and the sweet falling of the clauses, and the varying and illustration of their works with tropes and figures, than after the weight of matter, worth of subject, soundness of argument, life of invention, and depth of judgement'. That good humanist and disciple of Sir John Cheke, Thomas Wilson, was in no danger of neglecting *inventio* ('life of invention') and *dispositio* ('depth of judgement'), but other rhetoricians of his century —Sherry, Puttenham, Fraunce, Peacham, and Hoskins— confined the art of rhetoric almost entirely to *elocutio* or 'the varying and illustration of works with tropes and figures'. It is not necessary to go to Pettie or Lyly to illustrate this addiction to tropes and figures, and especially to figures of sounds. The titles of some sixteenth-century works, all entered in the Stationers' Register, are suggestive: *A delicious syrup newly clarified for young scholars that thirst for the sweet licour of Latin speech*; *A translated tantara of transitories present and terrors to come*; *The chips of salvation hewed out of the timber of faith*. Agnomination, isocolon, antithesis of words rather than of thought, these and other word-schemes are epidemic in the prose of that period. Here are two examples in which it is not easy for a modern reader to detect the language of passion. First, the opening sentences of a love-letter, now in the Bodleian Library, written a few months after the publication of *Euphues*:

'As the sailor that coveteth the fruition of a pleasant haven must prepare himself to endure many storms of the seas and many contrary winds of the air before he attain the wished port; and as the soldier that desireth to win a fenced fortress must arm himself to suffer many encounters, both by dint of sword and shot of cannon, before he get the desired victory; right so, whosoever he be that undertaketh the purchasing an unfained friend, a second self, a loving wife, must forthink to be withstood of that desire both by crossings of adverse chances, as it were with tempests, and vain yea vile reports, as it were blasts, yea expose his health and life to cares as it were to cannons, to griefs as it were to wounds, before he must once presume to suppose he shall achieve his enterprise; and content himself with this supposal that the end of his painful labour will be delight, as it were a haven wherein he shall rest, and a sure castle fenced to withstand all the force of furious adversaries or any chance whatsoever.'

And that this style was thought as suitable for haters as for lovers, we may gather from this passage from a 'sharp and vehement letter' (as John Foxe calls it) in which Lady Jane Grey—pupil of John Aylmer—reproaches Thomas Harding for recanting to Romanism at the beginning of Queen Mary's reign:

'I cannot but marvel at thee, and lament thy case, . . . thou which sometime wast the lively member of Christ, but now the deformed imp of the devil; sometime the beautiful temple of God, but now the stinking and filthy kennel of Satan; sometime the unspotted spouse of Christ, but now the unshamefast paramour of Antichrist; sometime my faithful brother, but now a stranger and apostata; yea sometime a stout Christian soldier, but now a cowardly runaway.'

If we place beside this stiff formalism a Jacobean passage on the same theme, we may think the formalism as stiff, but it is a formalism that has exchanged amplification for brevity. For this reason it will not be necessary to quote

more than a snatch from Joseph Hall's epistle to a 'revolted'
Protestant printed in 1608:

'Alas! what shall we look-for of you? Too late repentance,
or obstinate error? Both miserable. A *Spira*, or a *Staphylus*?
Your friends, yourself, shall wish you rather unborn, than
either.'

Hall in 1608 was a rising man in the Church, though he had
to wait for his bishopric till 1627. In 1597-8 he had published his *Virgidemiarum*, three books of 'toothless' satires
and three of 'biting', in which he claimed to be the first
English satirist, that is, the first to write satire after the
manner especially of Juvenal and Persius. He continued
to keep himself in the van of literary fashion. His *Characters
of Virtues and Vices* (1608) is the earliest collection of characters in English. More didactic than most of those that
follow, it is not 'wit's descant on any plain song' as in Overbury and his circle, but an attempt to give to the characters
of Theophrastus and the teaching of the classical moralists
—'the divines of the old heathens'—a Christian flavour.
And the heathen divine who is most to Hall's taste as
moralist and stylist is Seneca. The justice of the label
which became attached to him—'our English Seneca'—is
yet more apparent in his *Epistles* (1608 and 1610): 'a new
fashion of discourse, by Epistles; new to our language,
usual to others'. Here, as Seneca to Lucilius, he attempts to
be free and familiar—'we do but talk with our friends by
our pen, and express ourselves no whit less easily; somewhat
more digestedly'—but at the same time full of profitable
matter. He was called 'our English Seneca', says Fuller,
'for his pure plain and full style', perhaps also because like
'our Lipsius' he found in stoicism—a Christian stoicism—a
refuge from times which, as he held, exceeded all others in
evil. In theology he kept to the beaten road of the Church
and rejected all singularity, whether that of Arminius or of

the separatists of Amsterdam; and in prose-style he affected a Senecan gravity and fullness without singular paradoxes or points of wit and without coveting brevity to the point of obscurity, a style that is nearer to South than to Andrewes. Ingenious images are not sought after. Oddly enough, the most striking in the *Epistles* has escaped the notice of Donne's commentators. To the age of Hall and Donne the image would not appear so striking or so ingenious as it does to us; and it could only appear absurd to an age like Johnson's that had ceased to attach much value to allegory and emblem except for purely didactic purposes. If we accept Walton's dating of 'Valediction: forbidding mourning' (1611), this was printed three years before Donne wrote his poem:

'An heart truly faithful cannot but have an hand Christianly bountiful: Charity and Faith make up one perfect pair of compasses, that can take the true latitude of a Christian heart: Faith is the one foot, pitch't in the centre unmovable, whiles Charity walks about, in a perfect circle of beneficence: these two never did, never can go asunder.'

When Milton attacks Hall for making sentences 'by the statute, as if all above three inches long were confiscate', a Ciceronian is attacking a Senecan; Milton's rejection of Senecanism in prose is almost as unusual in his time as his rejection in poetry of the 'trimmings slight' that 'take our late fantastics with delight'.

As I have taken from Hall examples of the cult of Senecanism, so I may take from a passage in another small writer, Sir William Cornwallis, an example of the anti-Ciceronianism which accompanied it. Perhaps he has in mind Montaigne's confession that while he found Seneca 'full-fraught with points and sallies' and Plutarch 'stuffed with matters' he found in Cicero for the most part nothing but wind and ostentation. It will be noticed that Corn-

wallis is as self-conscious as Hall in detaching himself from
the old style.

'Words . . . are but the Lackies of reason of which, to send
more than will perform the business is superfluous. Methinks
an *esse videatur* at the close of a period is as nice as a Tumbler
ending his tricks with a caper: and Tully's *Venit, imo in senatum
venit* moves me no more against Catiline than the first *Venit*.
Methinks this same rhetoric the child of words is but as a
pickled herring to bring on drink, for his divisions and repetitions are for nothing but to bring his memory acquainted with
his tongue and to make three works of one. How shall a man
hope to come to an end of their works, when he cannot with
two breaths sail through a Period, and is sometimes gravelled
in a Parenthesis? I wonder how Cicero got the people of Rome
tied so fast to his tongue, for which his matter, no better than
his style, he should not persuade me to look upon him. I make
as great difference between Tacitus, Seneca's style, and his,
as musicians between *Trenchmore* and *Lachrymæ*. Methinks the
brain should dance a jig at the hearing a Tullian sound, and
sit in counsel when it hears the other . . . eloquence (as we take
eloquence) it is of no use, but among such ears as call a bag-
pipe music: it fits them, and among them must be used; but
among wise men it is to distrust their understandings, losing
time in repetitions and tautologies. The virtue of things is not
in their bigness, but quality, and so of reason which wrapped
in a few words hath the best tang.'

The attack is not merely on Ciceronianism as was that of
Erasmus, but also upon Cicero himself and his *eloquentia*,
and Cornwallis is but a minor figure in a revolution which,
as Professor Croll has shown, had profound effects upon
the vernacular literatures of Europe and not least upon
English prose in the seventeenth century. The opposition
of Muret and Lipsius, Montaigne and Bacon, to Cicero
and his imitators had been positive and constructive. They
looked for a style that should be more in keeping with the

spirit of free inquiry into the morals of men or the secrets of
nature which they desired, a style that preferred intimate
discourse to public oratory, one that could stop and brood,
present the mind in process of meditation, turn upon itself
to hint a doubt, indicate that knowledge was not yet a
circle, a style that whether terse or loose would avoid
copiousness and place matter before words. The Ciceronian Ascham had said: 'Ye know not what hurt ye do to
learning that care not for words but for matter', and while
the insurgents cannot be said to take exactly the opposite
view—for they too were intensely interested in words—
very deliberately they put matter first and the problem of
communicating matter. Their models they found in the
Silver Latin writers, above all in Seneca and Tacitus and
the younger Pliny, nor is it a solecism to add Plutarch and
Epictetus, since the age read the *Moralia* and the works of
Epictetus in Latin translation.

No Englishman of his day was more concerned with the
problems of communication than that good European
Francis Bacon, or left behind him in print or manuscript
so much evidence of his concern. The whole bent of his
mind being set upon *fructus*, it is not surprising that his
treatment of poetry (answering to imagination) in the
second book of *The Advancement of Learning* is but a brief and
unsatisfactory interlude between his treatment of history
(answering to memory) and philosophy (answering to
reason). Poetry, by which he means narrative and allegorical fiction, 'doth raise and erect the mind, by submit-
ting the shews of things to the desires of the mind'; it is an
escape from the disappointing realities of life to an ideal
world where actions are more heroical, the virtuous are
rewarded, and the vicious punished; but prose, being
obedient to the laws of reason, 'doth buckle and bow the
mind unto the nature of things'. Like Sir Henry Savile he

seems to have thought poets the best writers next to them that wrote prose, and it is with obvious relief that he passes from imagination to reason. But Bacon was too clear-sighted to suppose that men could live by reason alone. He knew that eloquence prevailed in an active life, and he was not so Senecan as to be willing to dispense altogether with Cicero, like the retiring Stoic, Cornwallis. The active life appealed to him as much as the contemplative life. We do not feel about him as we feel about More that but for the call of duty he would have preferred to live the life of a philosopher with Hythloday rather than take his part in public life in the hope, if not of turning things to good, yet of so ordering them that they might not be very bad. Bacon can say without a struggle: 'It is reserved only for God and angels to be lookers on'; and he would have sympathized with Quintilian's desire to mould the 'Romanum . . . sapientem, qui non secretis disputationibus, sed rerum experimentis atque operibus vere civilem virum exhibeat'. And so the lawyer and statesman, and preacher of the gospel according to observation and experiment, has at times recourse to the eloquence of persuasions, as in the passage on the durability of learning I have already quoted, an eloquence or rhetoric that 'applies reason to imagination for the better moving of the will'.

It is remarkable to what lengths Bacon went to have knowledge digested and ready for use. The story is told of a man who had so brilliant an idea that he went down on his knees to thank God for it, and when he rose found that he had forgotten it. Bacon took no such risks. When a notion darted into his mind, he or a secretary (say, Thomas Hobbes) wrote it down, so that it remained within call and ready for use. We may take as an example his Promptuary or preparatory store which he drew upon for many of his essays. To this belong his analysis of the sophisms of popular

argument—the *Colours of Good and Evil*; his *Antitheta* or
brief arguments drawn up in the form of a balance-sheet
for or against such frequently recurring themes as riches,
wife and children, love, revenge, dissimulation, to be used
in proof and refutation, persuasion and dissuasion, praise
and blame; his *Formulae Minores* of which the *Promus of
Formularies and Elegancies* is an example, with its metaphors,
quotations, proverbs, analogies, antitheses, neat transi-
tions, telling retorts, complimentary phrases; his *Apoph-
thegms* or historical *exempla* of pointed and witty sayings—
'*Mucrones Verborum*, Pointed Speeches. Cicero prettily calls
them *Salinas*, Salt-pits.' These stores and no doubt many
that have perished are not mere transcriptions or borrowings from books but, like Jonson's *Discoveries*, bear the
impress of his mind and character. So, too, do his remarks
upon the methods of communication, which vary with the
subject-matter and the audience. The distinction which he
draws between the magistral and the initiative suggests the
distinction between Ciceronian oratory and Senecan discourse; the one teaches knowledge to the crowd of learners
and requires that what is told should be believed, and the
other intimates and insinuates knowledge to the few in the
same form in which it grew in the mind and requires that
what is told should be examined. Not very different
appears the distinction between the delivery of knowledge
in methods and in aphorisms, methods exhibiting knowledge in orb and circle as if it were already complete, and
aphorisms representing fragments of knowledge and invit-
ing others to add something in their turn to its sum. That
Bacon with his high contemplative aims would prefer the
initiative or aphorisms—the form which he gave to the
Novum Organum—is to be expected, for 'eloquence is doubt-
less inferior to wisdom'; that Bacon with his grasp of what
men do and are would realize the importance of the

magistral or methods—the form which he gave to *The Advancement of Learning*, Book I—is also to be expected, for 'in profit and in popular estimation wisdom yields to eloquence'.

In aphorisms, Bacon says, illustration, variety of examples, connexion, descriptions of practice are omitted and what remains is some good quantity of observation, so that a man will hardly think of using this form unless he is solidly furnished for the work. This form it was that he used for those 'fragments of my conceits', the ten essays of 1597. It would not seem possible that English prose could be more condensed than it is here: the *brevitas* of Tacitus and Lipsius can go no farther in our language. John Hoskins of the Middle Temple probably has Bacon and Lipsius in mind as well as Seneca when about the year 1599 he attacks the 'short-breathed gentlemen' who write all in 'sentences' and all sententiously. '*Sententia*, if it be well used, is a figure—if ill and too much, it is a style. . . . Whilst moral philosophy is now a while spoken of, it is rudeness not to be sententious. . . . It is very true that a sentence is a pearl in a discourse; but is it a good discourse that is all pearl? . . . Why should the writers of these days imprison themselves in the straitness of these maxims?' And he goes on to quote Caligula on Seneca: 'It makes their style like *arena sine calce*.' Whether Bacon realized that he had carried aphorism too far, whether he had been surprised by the popularity of his essays and felt that a less esoteric style was demanded, whether he had come to see greater possibilities in the essay form especially for a man like himself so nimble and versatile in catching the resemblances of things, for whatever reason or reasons, in the essays of 1612 and 1625 he adds more and more lime to his sand. His style remains aphoristic rather than magistral, but now he mortises the joints of his dispersed meditations together with connecting particles, freely admits metaphor, simile, example, analogy, and proverb, and with the enrichment of trope and figure comes the enrichment of cadence until he arrives at such splendour as: 'It is heaven upon earth, to have a man's mind move in charity, rest in providence, and turn upon the poles of truth.' The sixteenth century had been fond enough of 'sentences', but Bacon's reflections upon the moral or immoral nature of man sting the reader into thought with images unexpected and sometimes startling, language so condensed that it compels attention, and cadences that do not dull the ear with uniformity. We may get some inkling of the effect which his 'sentences' had upon some contemporaries from Owen Felltham's rhapsody on reading 'a rarely sententious man': 'I cannot read some parts of Seneca above two leaves together. He raises my soul to a contemplation which sets me a thinking on more than I can imagine. So I am forced to cast him by and subside to an admiration.'

In one of the few passages added in the Latin translation (1623) of the first book of *The Advancement of Learning* Bacon dissociates himself, as he could not so decently have done in 1605, from a vanity of style which he had come to think little better than the 'copy' and superfluity of speech which it had succeeded, a style in which

'the labour is altogether that words may be aculeate, sentences concise, and the whole contexture of the speech and discourse rather rounding into itself than spread and dilated: so that it comes to pass by this artifice that every passage seems more witty and weighty than indeed it is. Such a style as this we find more excessively in Seneca; more moderately in Tacitus and Plinius Secundus; and of late it hath been very pleasing unto the ears of our time.'

Clearly Bacon believed himself guiltless of this vanity; and proof of his innocence may be found in *The History of Henry the Seventh* (1622). Yet if in this work he shows no wish to imitate the style of Tacitus, he also shows that his admiration for Tacitus as moralist and historian has not diminished with the years. (Much of Tacitus he could and did absorb through Machiavelli and Lipsius, but he goes also to the fountain-head.) The times he chose to depict were not sombre and repulsive like those of his master, nor was Bacon by temperament a pessimist; but in his reflections on political expediency, in the skill with which he analyses the hidden motives of his characters, in the flashes of irony which light up from time to time the gravity of his narrative, we see where he had put himself to school. 'Vivas morum observationes spirat' is his splendid tribute to Tacitus: 'he utters the very morals of life itself'. When we consider how repeatedly Clarendon, too, turns to the same source for guidance and inspiration, may we not say that it was under the auspices of Tacitus that English history became adult?

To his attack on the Senecan vanity of style Bacon adds the words, 'by the more exact judgements it hath been deservedly despised', and among these more exact judgements is that of Bacon's friend Sir Henry Savile. If I speak of Savile on Tacitus, I shall be illustrating my statement that the Elizabethans never wrote better prose than in their translations and at the same time drawing attention to a neglected work. It is remarkable that no reprint of Savile's translations of the *Histories* and the *Agricola* (1591) has been published for more than two hundred years. Ben Jonson praised him for rendering Tacitus 'in all his bounds, And all his numbers, both of sense and sounds'. The compliment is well meant, but I am not sure that Savile relished it. Perhaps Anthony Bacon, who wrote the address to the Reader, gets nearer to the intention of Savile's translation:

'Tacitus . . . hath written the most matter with best conceit
in fewest words of any Historiographer ancient or modern.
But he is hard. *Difficilia quae pulchra*; the second reading over
will please thee more than the first, and the third than the
second. And if thy stomach be so tender as thou canst not
disgest Tacitus in his own style, thou art beholding to Savile,
who gives thee the same food, but with a pleasant and easy
taste.'

Savile's style is certainly easier and pleasanter than Richard
Greneway's in his translation of the *Annals* (1598), a work
'ignorantly done', as Jonson says, which sometimes reads
like a bad crib. ('Whilst these things thus passed, Caesar
having deeply thought upon, and after protracted his
determination, at last goeth into Campania.') Savile,
while hoping that Tacitus might yet retain in his translation something of his former strength and much of his
substance, realized that the English language was 'not so
fit to set out a piece drawn with so curious a pencil'. Nor is
he thinking merely of the impossibility of rendering in
English the *imperatoria brevitas* of Tacitus. He was translating just before the imitation of Seneca and Tacitus had
become fashionable in England, but at any time in his life
he would have thought Tacitus's 'pencil' in some respects
too 'curious'. A passage at the end of his annotations
on the *Agricola* deplores the 'sophisticate eloquence, and
rhyming harmony of words, whereunder was small matter
in sense, when there seemed to be most in appearance . . .
induced into Graecia . . . found favour in some corners
of Asia . . . begun [among the Romans] by Seneca, Quintilian, the Plinies, and Tacitus . . . and lastly conveyed
to Christian religion by Cyprian, Ambrose, Augustine,
Bernard, &c.' Savile makes no attempt to preserve Tacitus's rhetorical devices, and the effect of the brilliant
epigrams which his author is as careful to place as to phrase

is quite lost; but the grave and tender paragraphs with which the *Agricola* closes retain in Savile's expanded (but not dilated) version a solemn music.

'If there be any place for the ghosts of good men, if, as wise men define, the souls of great persons die not with the body, in peace mayest thou rest, and recall us thy posterity from impatient and womanish wailings to the contemplation of thy virtues, which are in no sort to be sorrowed for, or bewailed, but rather admired. . . . This is true honour indeed, and this is the duty of nearest kinsfolks. So I would counsel thy daughter and wife to reverence the memory of their father and husband with often remembering his doings and words, recognizing the glory and image of his mind rather than of his body: not that I dislike of images cut in marble or metal, but as men's faces, so the images of faces are mortal and frail; the shape of the mind is eternal, which we may represent and express, not by matter and art borrowed abroad, but by our own manners within. That of Agricola which we did love, which we admired, remaineth, and so will remain, in the minds of men, in the continual succession of ages, in fame and renown. For many of the ancients shall lie buried in obscure and inglorious oblivion, but Agricola shall live recommended to posterity, and continue for ever.'

Tacitus 'is hard. *Difficilia quae pulchra*'; and it was the difficulty and darkness that attracted some prose-writers and some poets. In that characteristic piece of Jacobean meditation, *Resolves* (c. 1623), Owen Felltham writes of poetry: 'One thing commends it beyond Oratory: it ever complieth to the sharpest judgements. He is the best Orator that pleaseth all; even the Crowd and Clowns. But Poetry would be poor, that they should all approve of. If the learned and judicious like it, let the Throng bray. These, when 'tis best, will like it the least.' Felltham is writing about poets and poetry, and in terms very similar to Chapman's well-known manifesto in the dedication to

Ovid's Banquet of Sense (1595): 'that Poesy should be as pervial as oratory, and plainness her special ornament, were the plain way to barbarism'. But as was usual in an age when criticism was still in the main directed by the *trivium*, by the rival claims of grammar, logic, and rhetoric, his remarks are as applicable to prose, terse anti-Ciceronian prose, as to poetry. Prose or poetry that was dark and difficult, whether from the obscurity of the matter or its compression or the writer's wit, came to be known as 'strong-lined', and the expression was used in praise or vituperation according to rhetorical taste. Perhaps we see the germ of the expression in Florio's Montaigne: 'My workmanship addeth no grace unto the matter. And that's the reason I must have it strong, with good holdfast, and shining of itself.' In Cornwallis, who had read parts of Florio's translation in manuscript by 1600, this use of 'strong' is clearly established. He is stating his preference for prose that shall be 'loose' rather than 'terse', and has one eye on the Tacitean curtness of Bacon's *Essays* of 1597: 'I hold neither Plutarch's, nor none of these ancient short manner of writings, nor Montaigne's, nor such of this latter time to be rightly termed Essays, for though they be short, yet they are strong, and able to endure the sharpest trial.' Examples from two famous books may be cited in both of which the sense tends to be pejorative. First, Burton in 'Democritus to the Reader': 'He respects matter, thou art wholly for words, he loves a loose and free style, thou art all for neat composition, strong lines'; and a little later he observes that he has written with as small deliberation as he ordinarily speaks, 'without all affectation of big words, fustian phrases, jingling terms, strong lines, . . . which many so much affect'. Again, in a famous passage in *The Compleat Angler* Walton praises 'that smooth song' Marlowe's 'Come live with me' and Raleigh's answer to it at the expense of 'the strong lines that are now in fashion in this critical age'. But *pace* Walton there are signs that by his time the date of strong lines was out, and for reasons of which he was not fully aware and of which he would strongly have disapproved, reasons not unassociated with the name of Hobbes and with the movement that led to the foundation of the Royal Society.

In the pamphleteers addressing themselves to a popular and unlearned audience we should not expect strong lines, and it is here that the best examples of the old copious rhetoric survive. The Jacobean pamphleteer Dekker differs from the Elizabethan pamphleteer Nashe not in rhetoric but in diminution of power and intelligence. He can indeed pull out the Senecan stop when it suits him to do so:

'Acquaint thyself therefore not with the most, but the best: not the best in clothes or money, but the best in doing best, or doing well. Are there none such in prison? Keep company then with thyself, and in thy chamber talk with Plutarch or Seneca: the one will teach thee to live well, the other to die well.'

But this concession to fashion is rare in him. When Cowley in his Ode 'Of Wit' describes what wit in 1656 was not— not

> a tall Metaphor in the bombast way,
> Nor the dry chips of short-lung'd Seneca—

he could have had Dekker in mind in the first line but not in the second. The image with Dekker is a favourite means of amplification. This we may see if we place beside the description of the tricks and devices of horse-dealers in *Lanthorn and Candlelight* (1608) the original which he borrowed without acknowledgement from Gervase Markham's *Cavelarice, or The English Horseman* (1607). Dekker tries to put mettle into Markham's plain and serviceable prose by dilating it with metaphors and allusions drawn from war, from popular entertainments (fencing, the theatre, tumbling, fireworks, and Bedlam), from trades and professions (barbers, physicians, painters, cheaters and swaggerers, monopolists, begging soldiers, and whores), from drink and tobacco, from articles of attire (cloaks and a ruffled boot) and of the house (a dial or time-keeper), and from such familiar sights as the kites and ravens that fed on carrion in London streets. Coleridge writes of the danger of thinking without images, but to a writer of Dekker's calibre the danger was not so much of thinking without images as of not thinking at all and of using images in and out of season in pursuit of amplification.

Still more popular than the pamphlet—for they did not necessarily make any demands upon literacy—were the sermon and the play. Of the play I shall speak in a later lecture; to say anything of the sermon in a few words I should need a more than Tacitean brevity. Burton refused to add to the number of sermons that poured from the press: 'a Sermon at Paul's Cross, a Sermon in St. Mary's Oxon, a Sermon in Christ Church, or a Sermon before the Right Honourable, Right Reverend, a Sermon before the Right Worshipful, a Sermon in Latin, in English, a Sermon with a name, a Sermon without, a Sermon, a Sermon, etc.', and the 'etc.' seems to stretch out to infinity. The variety is as bewildering as the quantity: sermons plain and coloured, Attic and Asiatic, simple and learned, dry and watery, rhetorical and dialectical; and while some distinction according to creed is possible, it cannot be clear-cut, for a Puritan might be terse or copious, might (with discretion) admit heathen embellishments or might not. Samuel Hieron of Eton and King's, Puritan incumbent of Modbury in Devonshire, attacks some vanities of preaching in his *Preacher's Plea* (1604): the preacher who descants upon every letter in his text, tossing it hither and thither, and offering it any violence to frame it to an imagined conceit; the preacher who mounts aloft to astonish the multitude, using great words and new coined phrases fitter for a tragedian than a minister of the gospel; the preacher who to gain the repute of a profound man 'rubbeth over the unsavoury writings of some moth-eaten friar' and amazes himself and his congregation with a multitude of allegories and intricate distinctions; the preacher who to gain the repute of a learned man interlaces his sermons with many shreds of Latin and Greek. Under which of these headings Hieron would have placed William Barlowe, Bishop of Rochester, I do not know; perhaps under them all. Five days after the discovery of Gunpowder Plot Barlowe preached a sermon at Paul's Cross on the well-chosen text: 'Great Deliverances giveth he unto his King, and sheweth mercy to his anointed David and to his seed for ever'. The place, the famous Cross, 'the most noted and solemn place', as Dugdale calls it, 'for the gravest Divines and greatest Scholars to preach at', the theme a plot sensational beyond any other in English history; yet in such a place, at such a time, and with such a theme, Barlowe preaches in this manner:

'In the part *intensive*, concur two parts; First, the double *quantity*, both that which they call *discreta*, the plurality of the number [*Deliverances*] as also that which they call *continua*, the magnitude thereof [*great*,] Secondly, the double quality, as well internal and essential [*salutes, healths, wholesome Deliverances*:] as outward and accidental, [*magnificasti*] *deliverances*, beseeming a *Great God*, whom Saint *Basil* calleth ἀξιωματι-κώτατον βασιλήα, a most magnificent King.'

This kind of needlework, we may believe, pleased the '*solertia* and ingeniosity of spirit' which Barlowe praises in his king, and perhaps on the principle of *omne ignotum pro magnifico* it pleased the illiterate members of his audience.

The variety of the seventeenth-century sermon is well shown by the differences between Donne and Andrewes, the most distinguished preachers of the High Anglican movement. Hieron might have addressed his remarks to either of them, though if he had fairly applied 'the rules of comeliness and correspondence' he would have allowed for the differences between the men of mean and middle rank, farmers and shepherds, for whom he wrote his 'homely and coarse discourse', and the critical audiences whom Andrewes addressed at Court and Donne in his cathedral of St. Paul's. Both Donne and Andrewes bring the whole weight of patristic and scholastic learning to bear upon the text and each word of the text, and when the meaning of a word seems utterly exhausted surprise us by extracting from it more new and unexpected meanings. Both are 'painful preachers', disliking loose sermons and scrupulously preparing their sermons for pulpit or for press; yet neither permits his learning to obscure the colloquial basis of his style nor allows his pains in preparation to destroy the impression that here is a man talking out his thoughts as they come to him. Both are 'strong-lined' men, believing that 'it fareth with sentences as with coins: In coins, they that in smallest compass contain greatest value, are best esteemed: and in sentences, those that in fewest words comprise most matter, are most praised'. Yet these two preachers, influenced by much the same models in sermon rhetoric, holding much the same doctrine, addressing often enough the same audience, exhibit great differences. Of the dramatic quality of Donne's work, where the stage is the pulpit, the actor the preacher, and the plot man's 'riddling, perplexed, labyrinthical soul'; of the subtle feeling for the texture of words; of the periodic structure of those passages in which he rises into eloquence, where the clauses as they ascend to their climax open out and close in so cunningly to capture the ear with the beauty of their varied rhythms; of these qualities, which have endeared Donne to the literary connoisseur and anthologist, there are few traces in Andrewes. Looked at from one point of view Andrewes's style reaches the height of Senecan vanity or the vanity of those Fathers of the Church whose 'sophisticate eloquence' Savile condemned. The 'points' which Andrewes found in the Fathers were the 'points' in favour with King and Court:

> When James the first, at great Britannia's helm,
> Rul'd this word-clipping and word-coining realm,
> No words to royal favour made pretence
> But what agreed in sound and clash'd in sense.
> Thrice happy he! how great that speaker's praise,
> Whose ev'ry period look'd an hundred ways.

Long before the century was out, quibbling with sense had gone out of fashion as completely as quibbling with words, and the paradoxical antithetical wit of Andrewes had become as distasteful as his crumbling of the text or the jerkiness of his style. Bishop Felton died in 1626, the same year as Andrewes, yet he is reported to have said: 'I had almost marred my own natural Trot by endeavouring to imitate his artificial Amble'; and remembering Andrewes's analogical surprises we may say without indecorum that his sentences seem to advance by jet-propulsion. Yet to condemn his sermons as models for young preachers is one thing; to read them as the revelation of a saintly mind is another. Here we may say is a blaze of fireworks; but it is not the preacher that is illuminated, but the essentials of the Christian faith. No man is spoken of by his contemporaries with greater reverence; and even upon the minds of the greatest gallants at court, we are told, a sermon from

him left behind a sting or *aculeus*. As in his master Mul-
caster there are no concessions to a lazy mind. Let the
attention wander for a moment and the argument is lost;
but if the reader give to each word its due weight and
timing, then his sermons still leave behind an *aculeus*. When
South preached on plainness of speech in 1668 he was
attacking the florid preaching of Jeremy Taylor more than
the witty preaching of Andrewes; but though no doubt he
would not have admitted it, the effect of the apostles'
preaching as he describes it is the effect of the sermons of
Andrewes:

'when men came from such sermons, they never commended
the preacher for his taking voice or gesture; for the fineness of
such a simile, or the quaintness of such a sentence; but they
spoke like men conquered with the overpowering force and
evidence of the most concerning truths; much in the words of
the two disciples going to Emmaus: "Did not our hearts burn
within us, while he opened to us the Scriptures?" '

It is a superficial judgement that patronizes the prose of
a man like Andrewes as 'quaint' and a shallow dilettantism
that reads the work of another great Jacobean divine
merely for bits of odd learning, pleasing quirks of fancy,
amusing eccentricities of style. There was nothing odd or
unusual to the age in the elaborate structure of *The Anatomy
of Melancholy*, and a parallel to the plethora of quotation
may be found in Lipsius on Politics, a cento of passages from
the classics knit together by the brief sentences which
Dallington calls 'Lipsius' soder'. In many ways Burton was
a man of remarkable moderation. He keeps to the middle
of the road even in that *via media* the Church of England.
He is neither Calvinist nor Arminian, neither Galenist nor
Paracelsian, neither Puritan nor Cavalier. In smaller ways,
too, his moderation reveals itself: let the people sing
and dance, have their puppet-plays, stage-plays, and what

sports and recreations they like best, so long as all is used
opportunely and soberly; in dress to be in the fashion is to
observe a mean between prodigality of attire and dressing
'like an old image in Arras hangings'; as for beer, 'the
middling is fittest'. What is odd or rather *sui generis* is
his 'extemporanean style', a style as seemingly casual as
Andrewes's, though 'loose' not 'strong', and sometimes
affecting a deliberate oddness, as he confesses, especially
when he is being 'merry, facete, and juvenile', as Wood
says he often was among the 'ancients' of Christ Church.
It takes its colour from the matter: 'now serious then light,
now comical then satirical, now more elaborate then
remiss, as the present subject required, or as at that time I
was affected.' It is seldom a numerous style, for his quotations break up rhythm. (We may contrast *Urn-Burial*
where quotation in the two or three places where it appears
is banished to the end of a paragraph.) Yet there are
passages where the momentum of his passion sweeps on
unimpeded by the quotations, the lists of nouns and
adjectives and verbs, the short-breathed clauses, which he
so much affects. Two passages come especially to my mind:
the attack on the rich man who is charitable in public and
miserly and cruel in private, where the bitter variations on
the refrain 'He cares not. Ride on!' assist the cumulative
effect; and in the section on religious melancholy the passage on the tyranny of preachers who insult over and
terrify men's souls with talk of

'election, predestination, reprobation *ab aeterno*, subtraction of
grace, preterition, voluntary permission, &c. by what signs
and tokens they shall discern and try themselves, whether they
be God's true children elect, *an sint reprobi, praedestinati, &c.*
with such scrupulous points, they still aggravate sin, thunder
out God's judgements without respect, intempestively rail at
and pronounce them damned, in all auditories, for giving so

much to sports and honest recreations, making every small
fault and thing indifferent, an irremissible offence, they so
rent, tear and wound men's consciences, that they are almost
mad, and at their wits' ends.'

Here Burton is weeping with Heraclitus; in the section on
love melancholy he laughs with Democritus and Lucian;
and sometimes, so mixed was his passion, he laughs and
weeps at one and the same time. Timothy Bright's *Treatise
of Melancholy* (1586), a mere professional performance, and
the livelier *Passions of the Mind* (1601) of Thomas Wright
are known only to historians of medicine and psychology,
but Burton's compassion for and insight into the perturbations of the mind, so much more grievous than those of the
body, can never become obsolete. We do not read far in
his book without meeting the words 'feral' (deadly, fatal)
and 'crucify'; his main theme is the feral diseases by which
man is crucified. One of the fathers of Salomon's House in
The New Atlantis 'had an aspect as if he pitied men'. Of no
Jacobean are the words truer than of Burton. He wrote his
book not merely to preserve himself from melancholy but
because he pitied men.

I began these remarks on the confused magnificence of
Elizabethan and Jacobean prose with some illustrations of
the extreme rhetorical formalism of mid-sixteenth-century
prose; I end by returning to Elizabethan prose for the
purpose of entering two caveats. The first is against supposing that all Elizabethan prose has the copiousness of
amplification to be observed in most pamphleteers or the
attention to parison and agnomination and *similiter cadens*
to be observed in the euphuists. The doctrine of decorum
or 'respect' (as Puttenham calls it) imposed the duty of
suiting the style to the theme and the audience, and led to
discrepancies in one and the same writer which we do not
find in modern prose, even in letters. Lyly's civil and

courtly *Euphues* hardly seems to be by the same author as
the railing, ribald pamphlet *Pap with a Hatchet* with which
he knocks the Marprelates on the pate. ('If here I have
used bad terms, it is because they are not to be answered
with good terms.') Lyly, however, whether writing 'high,
mean, or base', could never be plain. Other writers dis-
claimed the 'filed points' of rhetoric because they knew
that their matter was good and believed that plainness and
simplicity were as much to be preferred in style as in dress
and manners, that for the proving of their high argument
logic was a better tool than rhetoric. William Perkins,
whose influence on the Puritans of England and New
England was deep and durable, expounded the doctrines
of predestination, imputed righteousness, or eternal damnation with as much bareness and simplicity as the difficulty of his themes permitted. He possessed, says Hall, 'a
distinct judgement, and a rare dexterity in clearing the
obscure subtleties of the school, and easy explication of the
most perplex discourses'. In his *Reformed Catholic* (1598) he
stated with the utmost precision and economy of words the
points of agreement and difference in Catholic and Protestant belief, so that it drew from an adversary the tribute
that he had seen no Protestant book that contained more
matter delivered in better method. The method of this
Church of England Calvinist—though he would have
repudiated any label less than that of Christian—was
strictly scholastic. He was not concerned to show his
learning, though he had learning and believed learning to
be necessary to the preacher. Whether he was arguing
against sectaries or Catholics, he permitted no adornments
to interrupt the progress of his thought. Arguments are
supported by occasional quotations from the Bible and the
Fathers or (rarely) by some modern instance of sin and
punishment, but neither in text nor margin is there any

tincture of pagan learning or pagan philosophy. He could and did say with St. Paul: 'my speech and my preaching was not with enticing words of man's wisdom but in demonstration of the Spirit and of power.' His instruction to preachers was to make their sermons 'both simple and perspicuous, fit both for the people's understanding, and to express the Majesty of the Spirit'; and his works are addressed to a less learned audience than is the work of that greater Church of England Schoolman, Richard Hooker. But the matter of Canterbury is presented with no less clarity and concinnity than the matter of Geneva. And if something of the narrowness and rigidity of his doctrine has got into the phrasing and rhythms of Perkins, the clenched fist and never the open palm, we may see in the grace of Hooker's diction and the modulation of his clauses the earliest manifestation of that movement—'comely but not gaudy'—which was to produce the sermons of Andrewes, the beautiful neatness of George Herbert's poems, the decency of a Laudian church or of the community at Little Gidding.

That freedom from 'all new affected modes of speech, whether borrowed from the court, the town, or the theatre' which Swift praised in the writings of the country clergyman Hooker and the Jesuit Parsons is shared also by Perkins; and if we descend below the level of these writers we find that many an author, whether because he followed the principle of decorum or because he was unlearned in the terms of rhetoric, wrote the plain prose of instruction in such subjects as arithmetic, cookery, horse-breeding, or plain narrative in many a first-hand account of discovery and travel by sea and land. Those who are content merely to state matters of fact, especially important matters of fact, are almost immune from rhetorical fashions. The prose of the Anglo-Saxon chronicle can be matched through the centuries. As Sir George Walton is said to have reported in 1718: 'Sir, we have taken and destroyed all the Spanish ships and vessels which are upon the coast, the number as per margin'; or as a British general reported to his Prime Minister: 'The Orders you gave me on August 15, 1942, have been fulfilled. His Majesty's enemies, together with their impedimenta, have been completely eliminated from Egypt, Cyrenaica, Libya, and Tripolitania. I now await your further instructions'; so Sidney, writing to a family servant he suspected of prying, dropped the hieratic style of his *Arcadia* for plain downright English: 'Few words are best. . . . If ever I know you do so much as read any letter I write to my father, without his commandment, or my consent, I will thrust my dagger into you. And trust to it, for I speak it in earnest. In the meantime, farewell. From Court this last of May 1578.'

My second caveat is against the danger of supposing that, because rhetorical manner is so obvious in much Elizabethan writing, matter is therefore insignificant. In particular, injustice has been done to *The Faerie Queene* and the *Arcadia*. 'The whole inclination and bent of those times', says Bacon, 'was rather towards copy than weight.' 'Copy' there is in these romantic epics, but weight also. The *Arcadia* is an 'amatorious poem', but it is not 'vain', nor is it merely 'amatorious'.

'Their courage was guided with skill, and their skill was armed with courage; neither did their hardiness darken their wit, nor their wit cool their hardiness: both valiant, as men despising death; both confident, as unwonted to be overcome; yet doubtful by their present feeling, and respectful by what they had already seen. Their feet steady, their hands diligent, their eyes watchful, and their hearts resolute.'

Robert Dallington chooses Sidney's commendation of his Arcadian gallant—*he durst and knew*—as symbolizing all requisite virtues in a gentleman; and the same words are chosen by Sir John Hayward to praise the great Elizabethan soldier Sir Roger Williams, 'a man who both knew and durst'. No better motto or impresa could be chosen for Sidney himself. The words express in little that union of the valour of the medieval knight with the learning of the humanist which make up the ideal of the Renaissance gentleman.

IV

POETRY

TO that greater Elizabethan epic, *The Faerie Queene*, injustice has also been done. The remoteness of Spenser's diction, the diffuseness of the style, and the elaborate decoration led many to suppose that he was merely a painter of lovely pictures in which matter was insignificant and manner all important.

> Now hath fair *Phœbe* with her silver face
> Thrice seen the shadows of the nether world,
> Sith last I left that honourable place,
> In which her royal presence is enrold.

That is, says Tom Warton, 'It is three months since I left her palace'. But it is also the tradition of heroic poetry available to Spenser, the art of fashioning a gentleman, and that encyclopedic tradition of learning which inspired Gabriel Harvey's rebuke that Spenser did not know enough astronomy for a poet. How a poet can be a great poet who has nothing to say, however melodiously he says it, I do not know; yet there have been critics who wandering in the bower of poetical bliss are seduced by the sweetness of Spenser's verse into ignoring the way of life which it is the purpose of his verse to set forth. If Milton had taken Hazlitt's view of Spenser as a poet of escape, whose poetry lulls the senses 'into a deep oblivion of the jarring noises of the world, from which we have no wish to be ever recalled', he would never have spoken of him as 'our sage and serious poet' or found in him a kinship of spirit which he found in no other English poet. For a hundred people who quote Ben Jonson's 'Spenser in affecting the ancients writ no language', perhaps only one remembers that he continued: 'Yet I would have him read for his matter'.

'Yet I would have him read for his matter; but as Virgil read Ennius.' In insisting on matter and rejecting archaism, Jonson practised what he preached. When we think of his poetry we are apt to think only of the perfection of some of his lyrics: 'Drink to me only with thine eyes', or 'Queen and huntress, chaste and fair', or 'Still to be neat, still to be drest'. These differ from Elizabethan lyric mainly in the perfection of their form, so consciously sought and achieved, they are composed to music with 'all the Graces of the age' and 'relishes of rhyme', they are the poems that get into the anthologies, and they are models to Herrick and other Cavalier lyrists. But if this were all, how could we account for Dr. Johnson's remark that Ben's manner while differing in the cast of his sentiments resembled Donne's in the ruggedness of his lines, or how could we explain that to this day critics dispute whether certain poems were written by Donne or by Jonson? To Jonson as to Donne matter was more important than words and the management of the thoughts dictated the rhetorical form. Like Donne he avoided any language that might be called 'poetical'. Implied in his rebuke of Spenser is a distaste for language that is remote from life and a faith in 'language such as men do use' in non-dramatic poetry as in dramatic. Jonson's getting by heart certain verses about wine from *The Shepherd's Calendar* may be accounted for by extra-literary reasons; but not his getting by heart certain verses by Donne. It is significant that he chose for special commendation not the 'Valediction forbidding mourning', not 'The Good Morrow', not one of the lyrics secular and divine which have gone to the head of the twentieth century, but two epistles in decasyllabic couplets. The one is a wittily humorous plea to his mistress not to insist that he melt down his gold to make good the loss of her bracelet, an elegy shot through with satirical references to the poor abuses of the time and ending in a mighty curse upon the wretched finder, one of the few poems of Donne in which his genius for hyperbole is turned to humorous rodomontade. And the other is a couplet from a familiar letter on the calm which beset the Island voyagers of 1597, a couplet which with astonishing condensation and exactness describes a ship in a dead calm:

> No use of lanthorns; and in one place lay
> Feathers and dust, to-day and yesterday.

Not Donne catching 'in some close corner of his brain' those refinements of mind and feeling in which he surpasses in subtlety all English love-poets, and with which sometimes he perplexes the minds not only of the fair sex, but Donne the vivid realist and the witty and humorous satirist: for these things Jonson esteemed him the first poet in the world. If I am right, then Jonson's view that Donne wrote all his best poems before he was 25, that is by 1597, becomes intelligible.

We cannot say when Donne's earliest poems were written. He was 21 in 1593, yet none of his poems were printed before 1633 except the *Anniversaries*, the Elegy on Prince Henry, and the verses on Coryate. If they had been printed earlier their influence outside his immediate circle would have been felt sooner. I do not know of an earlier reference to his verse than a paraphrase of some lines from 'The Storm' which appears in John Manningham's Diary in 1603. Oddly enough the same lines

> so that we, except God say
> Another *Fiat*, shall have no more day

are quoted in 1607 in Dekker's *A Knight's Conjuring*. If a writer so incompatible with Donne as Dekker can quote from manuscript verses and praise them as the work of 'so

rare an English spirit', Donne's fame as a poet must by then
have been firmly and widely established.

His break with Elizabethan poetry is so marked that we
have continually to remind ourselves how early in the
fifteen-nineties what we may take to be his Juvenilia were
written. Trying to account for the break is no doubt as
complicated an affair as trying to account for life. Many
have mentioned the anti-Ciceronian movement of which I
have spoken and the scepticism which sometimes accompanied it; or an early dialectical training among men of a
'suppressed and afflicted religion'; or that whetstone of
wit, the society of young lawyers and men about town at
the third university of the realm, the Inns of Court; inci-
dentally, we must not forget to mention Donne himself and
the reaction to be expected from a man of his temperament
to a rhetoric too formalized, a lyric attitude too Petrarchan.
Sir John Harington, who died in 1612 but never ceased to
be an Elizabethan or to long for the great days of his
revered if formidable godmother, writes about the year
1594: 'The Queen stood up and bade me reach forth my
arm to rest her thereon. Oh, what sweet burden to my
next song. Petrarch shall eke out good matter for this
business.' Donne would have been as delighted if he could
have contrived to come so near the Presence, and might
have made poetical hyperboles of it, but he would not have
reached for his Petrarch to eke out matter for his adulation.

Perhaps he felt himself to be in something of the same
predicament in which poets were placed early in this
century. 'Serious rhyme,' wrote Robert Bridges in 1912,
'is now exhausted in English verse. . . . Milton's blank verse
practically ended as an original form with Milton. There
are abundant signs that English syllabic verse has long been
in the stage of artistic exhaustion of form which follows
great artistic achievement.' And he wonders if Synge was

not right in questioning whether 'before verse can be human again it must not learn to be brutal'. Bridges in his neo-Miltonics did not become brutal enough, but we know how other poets did indeed become brutal and how they escaped from the conventions of nineteenth-century poetry, as Donne escaped from the conventions of Elizabethan poetry, by experimenting with the 'amalgamation of disparate experience', by refusing to keep accent, and by returning to the idioms and rhythms of speech.

'To read Donne', says Coleridge, 'you must measure *time*, and discover the time of each word by the sense of passion.' The pauses as much as the emphases and the disturbances of the syntax are essential to the communication of the ardour of the poet's thought. We may say of Donne's poems, as Brightman says of Andrewes's sermons, that 'perhaps no one could read them aloud with effect who did not possess a considerable faculty of dramatic interpretation'; and no one can read them aloud or to himself who does not understand the flux of the thought and passion. If we look at so fine an Elizabethan lyric as that suggested to Nashe by the plague of 1593, the poem which contains the famous stanza

> Beauty is but a flower
> Which wrinkles will devour:
> Brightness falls from the air;
> Queens have died young and fair:
> Dust hath clos'd Helen's eye:
> I am sick, I must die.
>> Lord, have mercy on us!

we find not only that much of the effect of the poem depends on the associations of words like 'beauty' and 'Helen' but that the stanzas are linked together not by argument but by mood and theme, so that the six stanzas might be rearranged without destroying the poem. In the self-contained form of the sonnet the Elizabethans often proceeded, as Petrarch had done, by closely knit dialectical argument. What they had done and were doing in the sonnet, Donne does in the lyric. It is this 'sequaciousness', this follow-through of logic and passion, which makes it possible to say that George Herbert and Marvell (with all their many differences from Donne and from each other) belong to the same 'school' of poetry as Donne, and that Southwell and Crashaw do not.

'Matter, not words.' In this sense De Quincey called Donne the first very eminent rhetorician in English literature, using the word Rhetoric as 'laying the principal stress upon the management of the thoughts, and only a secondary one upon the ornaments of style'. Donne is as much of an individualist as Milton, and there is no poet with whom he is comparable. But others at the same time were beginning like him to lay the principal stress upon the management of the thoughts and were eschewing the more formal ornaments of style; unlike him, whose style and rhetoric seem fully formed in his earliest verses,

> Whose every work, of thy most early wit,
> Came forth example and remains so yet,

some of them exhibit the evidence of conversion. The contrast between Raleigh's verses in commendation of Gascoigne's *Steel Glass* (1576) and the surviving fragment of 'Cynthia' (*c.* 1593) is remarkable: the one exhibits the extreme rhetorical formalism and metrical monotony of pre-Spenserian verse and the other is knotted and gnarled with passion and thought. Like Donne, Raleigh wrote an answer to Marlowe's pretty pastoral, 'Come live with me and be my love', that 'smooth song' which Izaak Walton preferred to the 'strong lines' of later verse; but whereas Donne is not so much making a critical comment on pastoral lyric as reducing its conventions, as he so often reduces scholastic dialectics, to the pin-point of personal passion, Raleigh, gravely judicial, challenges this fiction of a golden age in the name of the transience of human joys and the approach of age and death.

> But could youth last, and love still breed,
> Had joys no date, nor age no need,
> Then these delights my mind might move
> To live with thee, and be thy love.

Raleigh is one of many poets who in the phrase of that proud professional Ben Jonson wrote poetry 'on the by'. He is the gifted amateur who turned to poetry above all in the great crises of his life. We must now abandon the belief that

> Even such is Time which takes in trust
> Our Youth, our Joys, and all we have, . . .

was composed the night before his death, though it may be true that in his last hours the concluding stanza of a poem on the cruelty of Time came back to his memory as a fitting commentary on the bitter tragedy of his life, and that he wrote it down in his Bible with the addition of the prayer:

> And from which Earth, and Grave, and Dust,
> The Lord shall raise me up, I trust.

But the surviving fragment of 'Cynthia' relates to the loss of the Queen's favour, as does the beautiful 'Walsingham'; and 'Give me my scallop-shell of quiet', another of several poems in which Raleigh turns for his allegory to the Middle Ages, with its appeal from the corrupt justice of England to 'heaven's bribeless Hall, Where no corrupted voices brawl' and where 'Christ is the King's attorney', was written under expectation of death after his trial for treason at Winchester. The sonnet on *The Faerie Queene*, in its way a refusal of Petrarchanism, links Raleigh with a poet whom he did much to encourage: the thought just fills the sonnet-

form, and the end is as strong as the beginning. 'The Lie'
cannot be pinned down to a particular occasion, but it
bears the mark of a man who in the spacious phrase of a contemporary was 'our English Ulysses . . . of Nature's Privy
Council, and infinitely read in the wide book of the world'.

Raleigh's was an enforced solitariness, and he did not
cease to resent it. Other poets of his age found solitariness
more congenial and were much influenced in style and
thought by the Stoic philosophers, old and new. There is
Sidney's friend, Fulke Greville, a man whose life was less
adventurous and glamorous than Raleigh's though hardly
less active, and between whose public life at Court and
whose private life of meditation as uttered in verse and
prose there is a striking cleavage. There are Chapman and
Daniel, both critics as well as poets to an extent only
exceeded in their age by Jonson. (The loss of Jonson's
treatise on Poetry expressed by way of a dialogue with
Donne and others is one of the major losses in the literature
of that age.) Of these the poet of whom critics have had
least to say in recent years is perhaps Daniel. He was not
a 'strong-lined' poet, not even in *Musophilus*, in the sense
that his friend Greville was, or Chapman, whose verse has
been described as a Hymn to Difficulty; and perhaps this
was in the mind of Robert Anton when he wrote in 1616:

> And moral Daniel with his pleasing phrase,
> Filing the rocky method of these days.

'Pure accents brief', 'well-languaged', 'exquisite pains and
purity of wit', these are among the respectful tributes of
contemporaries.

Daniel, who was dependent all his life upon the favour of
the great, felt none of the frustration of enforced inactivity
from which Donne suffered for so many years. His special
pleasure was to hibernate for months together in order to

'converse daily in my quiet with the best of the earth'. Moral philosophy did not save him from feeling acutely the buffets of Fortune, as is so clear from the anguish of soul suffered during the trouble over *Philotas*. It did not abate his desire, repeatedly expressed, that while England kept the tongue it had, so long might his name and work be kept from perishing—a desire which explains in part the earnestness of the *Defence of Rhyme*, for he who had used rhyme even in his Senecan plays had indeed given hostages to fortune. But the stoicism which sustained him in the endless agitation of life inspired some of the best meditative verse of his or any generation.

In Francis Davison's *Poetical Rhapsody* (1602) Daniel is praised for his three several sorts of poetry: lyrical in his sonnets to Delia, tragical in 'The Complaint of Rosamond' and the Senecan drama *Cleopatra*, and heroical in his *Civil Wars*. Daniel's own division is suggested by the line from Propertius—*Aetas prima canat veneres, postrema tumultus*—which he used in his first volume of 1592 containing 'Delia' and 'Rosamond', in the edition of 1594 to which he added *Cleopatra*, and in the *Civil Wars* of 1595. The sonnets to Delia, the work of his earliest youth, are devoted to 'veneres', but from this 'low repose' he was raised up 'To sing of State and tragic notes to frame' by his own ambition, by Sidney's sister, and perhaps by Spenser's prophecy of 1591 that he would excel not in 'love's soft lays' but 'In tragic plaints and passionate mischance'. His themes in the *Civil Wars*, as in his Senecan plays *Cleopatra* and *Philotas*, are the 'tumults' of the disordered state and the disordered mind.

The objection to most of the sonnets to Delia is not that Daniel is borrowing from Desportes and others but that he does nothing interesting with what he borrows. Shakespeare and Drayton can transform commonplace into

discovery, can reanimate it to mind and sense: 'So all my
best is dressing old words new'. But Daniel, who had (for
his age) so little power over image and lyrical incantation,
needed to start with some solid body of observation and
experience, and this he did in the *Civil Wars*, as also (thanks
in part to Plutarch) in *Cleopatra* and *Philotas*. The wars
between the houses of York and Lancaster were to him, as
Delia was not, a subject of the greatest gravity, worthy of
the heroic style, the heroic stanza (ottava rima), and the
heroic stanza-filling simile; and it recommended itself to
him as to Shakespeare because of his passion for order and
for the welfare of his country. Jonson's gibe was that there
was not one battle in all the book. The two men were 'at
jealousies' with each other, and Jonson, if he had read the
poem, must have forgotten the vivid descriptions of the
battle of Shrewsbury and of the death of Talbot and his
son at Castillon, where the cool element of Daniel's verse
takes on momentarily a bold Elizabethan extravagance:

> For, in their wounds, our gory swords shall write
> The monuments of our eternity.

But it is true that there is less action in this chronicle epic
than in Warner's *Albion's England* or Drayton's *The Barons'
Wars*; it is also true that there is more and subtler political
and moral reflection. This reflection upon the frailties of
greatness and the disorders of glory and ambition, which
helps to give body to the poem and to raise it above the
prosaic level to which it sinks when the poet becomes sub-
merged in the historical subject-matter, was prompted not
only by observation at home and during his travels in
France and Italy but by converse with Fulke Greville and
with others who lived yet nearer to the sources of power.
It was prompted, too, by much converse with 'the best of the
earth' in books; we may note, for example, that the year

before the poem was published the six books on Politics or
Civil Doctrine which Lipsius had extracted from ancient
writers had been translated by Daniel's friend, William
Jones. 'Ambition, faction and affections speak ever one
language, wear like colours, . . . feed and are fed with the
same nutriments', Daniel writes; and Plutarch and Machiavelli, Seneca and Lipsius, were all to him contemporary
historians.

> O Blessed Letters, that combine in one,
>   All Ages past, and make one live with all:
> By you we do confer with who are gone,
> And the dead-living unto counsel call:
> By you th'unborn shall have communion
> Of what we feel, and what doth us befall.

> Soul of the world, Knowledge, without thee, ·
>   What hath the Earth, that truly glorious is?
> Why should our pride make such a stir to be,
> To be forgot? What good is like to this,
> To do worthy the writing, and to write
> Worthy the reading and the world's delight?

Aut facere scribenda, aut scribere legenda. But Daniel is
worthiest to be read not when he is writing of the tumults
of disordered times and the passions of others but when he
is disclosing the form of his own heart in those 'poetical
essays', moral discourses, or epistles which he began to
publish from 1599. Spenser did not and could not foresee
the Daniel of *Musophilus. A Defence of Learning*, of the
Epistle to the Countess of Cumberland, or of the funeral
poem on his patron, that 'happy warrior' Charles Blount,
Earl of Devonshire. What appealed to Wordsworth in
these poems, and especially in the Epistle to the Countess
of Cumberland, was a strain of meditative morality 'more
dignified and affecting than anything of the kind I ever
read' and the purity of the style. The *genus humile*, the

natural dress of Daniel's mind, chosen by him for intimate discourse as also for his pastoral, *Hymen's Triumph*, occupies that middle or 'neutral' ground of which Coleridge writes as being common to verse and prose. Rejecting the fashionable figures of the day and wearing only the plain habit of truth, the style is so 'modern' that the stanza quoted by the Wanderer in *The Excursion* seems but for some archaism in the syntax to be no quotation at all:

> Knowing the heart of man is set to be
> The centre of his world, about the which
> These revolutions of disturbances
> Still roll; where all th'aspects of misery
> Predominate; whose strong effects are such
> As he must bear, being powerless to redress;
> And that unless above himself he can
> Erect himself, how poor a thing is man!

It would be interesting to compare Daniel's defence of learning with Bacon's of a few years later. There is much common ground: the durability of men's minds in books, the importance of learning and of learned men to the state, the belief that the universities given new heart might make voyages of discovery in the immense and boundless ocean of nature's riches. What is not in Bacon is Daniel's ardent faith in the power of poetry and in the English language not merely at home but perhaps on strange shores and 'in the yet unformed Occident'; the call to his country to return to 'our ancient native modesty'; and the uncompromising rejection of expediency, worldly honour, power, and ambition for an inner peace of the mind not to be shaken by fear or hope, vanity or malice.

Daniel's is not specifically a Christian ethic: in many respects he is *homo antiqua virtute ac fide* and owes as much to the classical moralists as to the New Testament. If we turn to religious verse we find that one kind is conspicuously absent in Elizabethan and Jacobean times and indeed long after. We learn from Walton that Donne caused his 'Hymn to God the Father' to be set to a grave and solemn tune and to be often sung to the organ by the choristers of St. Paul's. The poem made a possible libretto for a cathedral anthem, sung perhaps to that 'more curious music' which the Injunctions of 1559 permitted before and after Common Prayer, but it was as obviously unsuited to congregational use as are the poems of Herbert and Crashaw. The idiom of Donne's divine poems does not differ from that of his secular:

> Each Altar had his fire;
> He kept his love, but not his object: wit
> He did not banish, but transplanted it,
> Taught it both time and place, and brought it home
> To Piety, which it doth best become.

Herbert said of his own poems, and the words are as true of Donne's divine poems, that they presented 'a picture of the many spiritual conflicts that have passed betwixt God and my soul'; Donne and Herbert use poetry for their *preces privatae*. We contrast the eighteenth century when men like Isaac Watts, Addison, and the Wesleys expressed thoughts and feelings common to all men in words and rhythms intelligible and acceptable to all and sundry. But the reason why the eighteenth century, not the seventeenth, is a great age of English hymnody is not to be sought in a change in critical taste. If in the English Reformed Church Lutheranism had prevailed over Calvinism, the Church might have had hymns in plenty, might have taken over, as did the Lutheran Church in Germany, some of the old Office hymns of the Catholic Church, while translating their use from the choir to the congregation and their language from Latin into the vernacular. But Calvin distrusted all human compositions that were not metaphrases of the Scripture, and under the influence of his followers

Englishmen became for nearly two centuries singers not of hymns but of metrical psalms. The Injunctions of 1559 had indeed permitted the use of hymns before and after Common Prayer, and a few appeared in 'Sternhold and Hopkins' (1561); but with the exception of a version of *Veni Creator Spiritus* from the *Breviary*, these are little more than mnemonic aids to the Book of Common Prayer, and the titles of the earliest editions suggest that they were at first designed for private use. Many seventeenth-century hymns, like the attempts of John Cosin and Jeremy Taylor to restore to the English Church the heritage of Catholic hymnody which it had lost at the Reformation, are obviously for use in private devotions, and had little or no influence outside a narrow circle. The case of George Wither is different. He designed his *Hymns and Songs of the Church* (1623) for congregational use, and secured a patent that they should be bound up with copies of the metrical Psalter. But even if he had been successful in his fight with the Stationers' Company to make his patent effective, we may doubt if he could have imposed his hymn-book upon the Church. Not till early in the eighteenth century did the time become ripe for Watts in his *Hymns and Spiritual Songs* (1707) to establish the character of the English hymn.

The importance attached by Protestants to literalness is well illustrated by Henry Ainsworth's rejection of the famous version of the hundredth Psalm attributed to William Kethe. Leader of the English separatists at Amsterdam and a good Hebrew scholar, he published at Amsterdam in 1612 annotations on the Psalms and a metrical Psalter. In his hands the first stanza of the Old Hundredth became:

> Shout to Jehovah, all the earth.
> Serve ye Jehovah with gladness:
> Before him come with singing-mirth.
> Know that Jehovah he God *is*.

But he kept the tune we all know, a tune borrowed from Calvin's Genevan Psalter. Ainsworth's was not the only attempt to improve upon 'Sternhold and Hopkins', although some versions were inspired by very different motives. I take an example from Joseph Hall rather than from the better known versions of Sidney, Sandys, or Milton. In 1607 he metaphrased some of the Psalms into a style more agreeable to the 'full perfection' of English poetry in his own time than the 'rude and homely' verse of the Old Version. The usual metres, long, short, and common—metres which Watts in 1719 deliberately preserved—Hall attacked: 'I never could see good verse written in the wonted measures. I ever thought them most easy, and least poetical'; and when he uses long metre, he gets a different effect by shedding archaism, running the sense on from stanza to stanza, and tightening the structure of the line by ridding it of those doublets and unnecessary particles which are satirized in Bishop Corbet's epigram on Robert Wisdom:

> And patch us up a zealous lay,
> With an old *ever and for aye*,
> Or *all and some.*

Something of this appears from Hall's version of Psalm 10. Instead of Sternhold's

> Tush, God forgetteth this, saith he,
>   therefore I may be bold:
> His countenance is cast aside,
>   he doth it not behold.
> Arise, O Lord, O God, in whom
>   the poor man's hope doth rest:
> Lift up thy hand, forget not, Lord,
>   the poor that be opprest . . .

Hall gives us:

> God hath forgot (in soul, he says)
> He hides his face to never see.
> Lord God, arise, thine hand upraise:
> Let not thy poor forgotten be.

Those whose ears were accustomed to the easy sense and regular beat of the Old Version thought his verses harsh. To them he replied, as a good Jacobean would, that 'roundness' was not to be preferred to sense, that while he welcomed smoothness he did not affect it, for in a verse that aimed at something more than musical delight smoothness was 'the least good quality'. But like the efforts of other reformers his were in vain. Indeed, in spite of the appearance of the New Version of Tate and Brady in 1696, many a village church went on singing the Old Version well into the nineteenth century.

I do not apologize for speaking in a lecture on Elizabethan and Jacobean poetry about a kind of verse that affected the lives of so many Englishmen at home and abroad for more than two centuries; but I must admit that we should have to give poetry a wide interpretation if we wished to include all but a very few of the metrical psalms and the hymns of the period. Poetry is not necessary to them; there is no difficulty in imagining how impressive were even Ainsworth's versions whether sung in Amsterdam or on the *Mayflower* or in the earliest settlements of New England. If we turn to religious verse that is or may be detached from music and liturgy, we find that the seventeenth century and the last years of the sixteenth are distinguished from the first half-century that follows the Reformation by the number and importance of the devotional poems then written and published. If we omit *The Faerie Queene* as the work of a poet who drank as much from

Helicon as Jordan, we may not omit on this score the works of Joshua Sylvester, whether original or (from about 1590) translated from Guillaume de Salluste, sieur du Bartas, although they bring us no nearer to essential poetry than the metrical psalms. Sylvester turned deliberately from 'Love's loose sonnets and lascivious mirth' to 'Urania or the Heavenly Muse' and in 1598 pleaded with Spenser, Daniel, and Drayton to turn with him. (But Spenser had already made his 'retraction' in the Hymns to Heavenly Love and Beauty.) The patriotic and Protestant fervour, the usefulness of the *Divine Weeks and Works* as an encyclopedia of current views whether on the macrocosm and the microcosm and their correspondences or on the marvels of natural history and the wonders of science, the elaborate similes which bring the reader the latest popular news of geographical discovery or everyday life, the strident and fantastic wit, the copiousness of a work

> Wherein like former fluent Cicero
> (With Figures, Tropes, Words, Phrases, sweetly rare)
> Of Eloquence thou mad'st so little spare
> That Nile (in thee) may seem to overflow

—these ingredients may explain the popularity of the English Du Bartas in and long after his generation. Jonson's public testimonial to the worth of Sylvester's work differs, as testimonials sometimes do, from his private opinion, but the critic is still baffled by the hold which Sylvester had upon the youthful Milton and the youthful Dryden. Those who do not confuse poetry with piety may ask if there ever was a poet with such admirers who showed such insensitiveness to word and cadence as did Sylvester in the 'gravesweet warbles of his native style'. He abused his mother tongue as Du Bartas abused his; and his original verses are only worse than his translations because he showed in them (as Drayton said) such poverty of invention that he 'still wrote less in striving to write more'.

Put his work beside Sir John Davies's *Nosce Teipsum* (1599) and the difference is apparent between a versifier and a man who can use philosophy in the service of poetry. Of invention in one sense of that word Davies had no need, for his matter was supplied to him by the meditation of ages upon the law of nature, the nature of the soul, and the relation between the soul and the body. The merit of the work lies as much in the skill with which he adjusts the rhetoric to his poetical purposes as in the disposition of the matter and the temper of the argument. His argument is not for Protestantism against Catholicism—there is but one reference to the 'Old Devotion' and that a respectful one—but for the Christian view of the world; and it is conducted in a 'middle style' which shuns inversion and technical terms and is not afraid of the monosyllabic base of the language.

> If death do quench us quite, we have great wrong,
> Sith for our service all things else were wrought,
> That daws, and trees, and rocks should last so long,
> When we must in an instant pass to nought.

His muse is supple enough to pass from the rich decoration and exuberant fancy of that 'sudden, rash half-capriole of my wit', *Orchestra, or, a Poem of Dancing* (1596), to the comparative sobriety of *Nosce Teipsum*. In the earlier poem he had laid himself open to Jonson's charge that he wrote transposable verses, but now the impulse of argument moves steadily forward, illuminated but not checked by the simple images with which he illustrates his difficult themes. If the texture of the verse is often close, it is not so close that it presents any of the dark enigmas of meaning with which we meet in Fulke Greville's packed and gnomic verse; and if the style is not spare and precise as in Herbert's 'Church Porch' it is as free from the copious amplifications of mid-sixteenth-century verse as from the vague emotionalism which is the bane of so much later religious verse. Here is a poet who can argue in verse—and do it to music—as well as any man before Dryden. The reader misses the majestic reaches of wit and passion which Donne explores when handling similar themes in the two *Anniversaries*, but he misses also in Davies's simpler and more equable verse the strained hyperboles of the greater poet. Antithesis and paradox there are, but not more than are inevitable to any poet whose theme is Man, 'a proud and yet a wretched thing', the Fall which in giving to Passion eyes 'made Reason blind', the Soul which has beginning and no end, and Death which is counted as 'birth or gaol delivery'.

If we were to seek paradox and antithetical thought in the religious verse of this period, we should go above all to Giles Fletcher:

> A Child he was, and had not learn't to speak,
> That with his word the world before did make,
> His Mother's arms him bore, he was so weak,
> That with one hand the vaults of heav'n could shake,
> See how small room my infant Lord doth take,
>> Whom all the world is not enough to hold.
>> Who of his years or of his age hath told ?
> Never such age so young, never a child so old.

These lines from *Christ's Victory and Triumph* (1610) carry us forward to Crashaw's lines on the Magdalen's tears,

> Nowhere but here did ever meet
> Sweetness so sad, sadness so sweet,

and, like the later Cambridge poet, Fletcher with tender and reverential wit lavishes upon his sacred themes the conceits and sensuous imagery and decoration with which secular poets had worshipped Venus. But I must not linger, before turning to the religious lyric, over a poet whom it is as misleading to call, as not to call, a Spenserian, so much is he like his master, and so much unlike. The critic is not baffled by the hold upon the youthful Milton of Giles Fletcher, nor surprised that Milton, like Keats, should have learned first from a Spenserian before discovering Spenser.

The dearth of religious lyric in the sixteenth century becomes apparent if we turn to a good anthology of the century's poetry, like that of Ault or Hebel and Hudson or E. K. Chambers, or if we go to the full selection of devotional poetry of the reign of Elizabeth made by Edward Farr for the Parker Society in 1845. There is an abundance of moral and didactic verse in lyric stanzas urging the golden mean, the vanity of worldly pomp, or the fickle frowns of Fortune, but of religious lyric that is comparable in merit to the secular lyric of the century the anthologists can find almost nothing. The contrast with the fifteenth century and its splendour of religious lyric and carol and with the seventeenth century with the great names of Donne, Herbert, Vaughan, and others, is glaring. It is as if the distrust of Calvin for the 'enticing words of man's wisdom' had destroyed for a time the power or desire to express religious joy and sorrow in song, as if poets had to wait until his influence lay less heavy upon the English Church or a part of it. With few exceptions the anthologists can find nothing to their purpose until the turn of the century, or till after the turn, when we may suppose that Donne, Fulke Greville, Henry Constable (a Catholic), and Campion wrote their divine poems. But the exceptions are interesting, and it is of these rather than the better-known poems of the next century that I will speak.

And I mention first a poem which no anthologist cares
to omit:

> Hierusalem, my happy home,
>   When shall I come to thee ?
> When shall my sorrows have an end,
>   Thy joys when shall I see ?
>
> O happy harbour of the saints,
>   O sweet and pleasant soil,
> In thee no sorrow may be found,
>   No grief, no care, no toil. . . .
>
> Our Lady sings *Magnificat*
>   With tune surpassing sweet;
> And all the virgins bear their parts,
>   Sitting about her feet . . .
>
> Hierusalem, my happy home,
>   Would God I were in thee!
> Would God my woes were at an end,
>   Thy joys that I might see!

There are many variants and additions, and some reduce
the poem to the level of a Puritan ballad, but it seems certain
that the verses, first printed in 1601, were written by a
Catholic and take some of their inspiration from St. Peter
Damian's hymn *Ad perennis vitae fontem*. Another poem, not
chosen by the anthologists named, could by no amount of
manipulation or suppression have been turned to Protestant purposes:

> In the wracks of Walsingham
>   Whom should I choose
> But the Queen of Walsingham
>   To be guide to my muse?
>
> Then, thou Prince of Walsingham,
>   Grant me to frame
> Bitter plaints to rue thy wrong,
>   Bitter woe for thy name . . .

Bitter, bitter, oh to behold
  The grass to grow
Where the walls of Walsingham
  So stately did show . . .

Level, level with the ground
  The towers do lie,
Which with their golden glittering tops
  Pierced once to the sky.

Where were gates, no gates are now,
  The ways unknown,
Where the press of peers did pass
  While her fame far was blown . . .

Both poems have the advantage of being settled in ancient and good traditions, the Latin hymn and the ballad. It is to be remarked that in one age the old Walsingham theme should have inspired two such fine yet discrepant poems as Raleigh's allegorical love poem, 'As you came from the holy land Of Walsingham', to which I have already referred, and this lament. Its authorship is unknown, and if it were known perhaps we should not be much the wiser; for we may have here the case of an untutored writer whose muse once only urged him to fill a popular form with bitter sorrow.

There is one known Catholic poet of the sixteenth century whose religious verses antedate those of the more famous Anglican writers of the next century. Robert Southwell's poems were published in London in 1595, but we do not know at what time in his life they were written between 1578, the year of his reception as a noviciate into the Society of Jesus, and 1595, the year of his martyrdom at Tyburn. His verses like his life were wholly dedicated to devotion. A poet of the Counter-Reformation, he determined to 'weave a new web' in the loom of the secular poets, and in his one long poem, 'Saint Peter's Complaint', he detains his theme, as Luigi Tanzillo had done in *Le Lacrime di San Pietro*, with sensuous images and with conceits of word and thought. In some respects it is the poem of one who 'banishing myself from the scene of my cradle in my own country' had lived 'like a foreigner, finding among strangers that which, in my nearest blood, I presumed not to seek'. Outside Crashaw's 'The Weeper', a poem which springs from the same tradition, there is nothing in English verse comparable to the twenty odd stanzas in which with 'disordered order' (a characteristic phrase and figure of Southwell's) St. Peter in his remorse describes the eyes of Christ (Luke xxii. 61–2). It is a little ironical that much of what Southwell reclaimed for devotional poetry in this and other poems returned to secular poetry in the thefts of Griffin's sonnet-sequence of 1596, *Fidessa*. In his shorter poems Southwell writes more in the English tradition, but in one that had become outmoded long before 1595. Reading Southwell, we might suppose that Spenser and Sidney had not yet transformed the character of English verse; did he find their doctrine too repulsive for their poetry to give him pleasure? The reflective verse of Sidney's friend, Sir Edward Dyer, one of the earliest of the Elizabethan court-poets, was more congenial, and he transposed Dyer's 'Fancy' into 'A Sinner's Complaint', and in 'Content and Rich' took hints from Dyer's 'My mind to me a kingdom is'. Southwell's lyrical ardour is too often smothered by the formal rhetoric and diction of the dull tradition in which he was writing; it flames out most brightly in the poems addressed to the infant Christ, 'New Heaven, New War', 'A Child my Choice', 'New Prince, New Pomp', and 'The Burning Babe' so much admired by Jonson. The last three are in the same metre; for although 'The Burning Babe' is usually printed in fourteeners, it breaks up easily into simple ballad measure (eights and sixes). Between the Reformation and Southwell I should not know where to look for this poetry of the *praesepe* outside the *Psalms, Sonnets, and Songs* (1588) set to music by another Catholic, William Byrd, where a carol with the traditional refrain

> Lulla la, lullaby!
> My sweet little baby,
> What meanest thou to cry?

appears beside a discreetly veiled poem on the martyrdom of Edmund Campion. The initial paradoxes of Christ's life provide the material for these poems of Southwell's.

> Weigh not his crib, his wooden dish,
>   Nor beasts that by him feed;
> Weigh not his mother's poor attire,
>   Nor Joseph's simple weed.
>
> This stable is a prince's court,
>   This crib his chair of state;
> The beasts are parcel of his pomp,
>   The wooden dish his plate.
>
> The persons in that poor attire
>   His royal liveries wear;
> The Prince himself is come from heaven,
>   This pomp is prized there.

This is from 'New Prince, New Pomp'. 'The Burning Babe' stands a little apart with its sustained conceits and dramatic setting; but in all four poems the language and rhythm are bare and simple, Christ's humanity and divinity are reconciled, and incongruity is compelled into congruity.

What I have said in this lecture on Elizabethan and Jacobean poetry has been necessarily partial. If in a coda it were possible to make some slight amends for the more serious omissions by describing the work of a man who was both Elizabethan and Jacobean and who in the course of a long life touched and adorned almost all the kinds of poetry practised in both generations, then there is no poet who would serve my purpose so well as Michael Drayton. To call the roll of his early poems is to indicate the prevailing kinds of poetry in their time. His versatility is apparent even in 1591, when he published metrical versions from the Old Testament and the Apocrypha of passages which range from the song of Deborah and the lamentations of Jeremiah to a complete version of the Song of Solomon in which none of the sensuousness (though much of the beauty) of his original is lost. In the nine eclogues of *Idea. The Shepherd's Garland* (1593) he shows himself an admirer of Sidney and of Sidney's sister—who shares with Lucy Countess of Bedford the title of patroness general of her age —shows himself, too, a disciple of Spenser and Chaucer with much of Spenser's diction and rhetoric and a touch of Chaucer's realism and raciness. (Still in 1619 he thought *The Shepherd's Calendar* 'a master-piece, if any' and Spenser the prime pastoralist of England.) But he is too near his models, as he is also in his sonnet-sequence of 1594, *Idea's Mirror*. If Shakespeare's sonnets are, as Keats said, 'full of fine things said unintentionally—in the intensity of working out conceits', that is not yet true of Drayton. Was it because of his great sensibility to the work of others, to Daniel and Du Bartas as well as Sidney and Spenser, that he developed late ? Imitativeness, a facility for rhetorical inflation, a weakness in design, and a too robust appetite for facts, these are all too evident in such 'Complaints' as *Piers Gaveston* (1593–4) and *Matilda* (1594), his chronicle epic *The Barons' Wars* (1603), and still more its earlier version *Mortimeriados* (1596). The figures which most easily beset him are strings of *sententiae* which skirt the edge of popular proverb and such accumulation as

> Thou base desire, thou grave of all good hearts,
> Corsive to kindness, bawd to beastly will,
> Monster of time, defrauder of deserts,
> Thou plague which dost both love and virtue kill,
>   Honour's abuser, friendship's greatest ill

in description of the power of gold. Amplification is less out of place in that pretty piece of paganism *Endymion and Phoebe* (1595), for the theme lends itself (as Keats found) to opulent decoration, and the ten-syllabled couplet does not tempt him, as do the stanzas of his historical poems, to pursue a figure to death; and in *England's Heroical Epistles* (1597), his most popular work, both the couplet and the semi-dramatic form exercise a salutary control.

By 1603, then, he had written—in addition to dramatic hackwork for Henslowe—sacred verses, sonnets, pastorals, 'complaints', heroical epistles, chronicle epic, had appeared as lyric poet in *England's Helicon*, and had begun his laborious 'chorography' of England and Wales, his *magnum opus* as he hoped it would be, his *Poly-Olbion*. His muse was indeed a maid-of-all-work. Nor does a list of his poems exhaust the tale of his labours, for all his life he busied himself, as perhaps no other English poet, in revising and even recasting old poems.

> All times and everywhere
> The Muse is still in ure.

Yet if Drayton had died in 1603, at the age of 40, he would have lived with narrow fame. Nor, as I have implied, is the neglect of his narrative verse entirely due to the reluctance of most modern readers to read historical narrative in verse or fictitious narrative in any form but the novel. After the turn of the century he continued, indeed, to have his failures, among them his satires and especially his poems on biblical themes, but in middle age a new access of power

came to him and it was not exhausted in old age. It did not
come to him in the form of a new vision, for he clung to the
old ways in poetry and continued to think of himself as the
heir of Spenser and Sidney, but it came to him in an assured
control over matter and rhetoric. He had his successes not
only in his 'odes' like 'To the Virginian Voyage' and 'The
Ballad of Agincourt' (1606) and such 'elegies' (1627) as the
familiar epistle to Henry Reynolds on 'poets and poesy'; he
succeeded also in kinds where on the whole he had failed
before, in the sonnet and the pastoral. That he could
succeed also in the long historical poem is shown by one
poem and one poem only, *The Battle of Agincourt* (1627).
The swift onrush of action and the economy of form are in
remarkable contrast to the leisurely progress of his earlier
work. This poem succeeds, however, only because it ex-
cludes so much: all character interest and all political and
moral reflection. For the modern reader the heroic spirit
which he wished to present to an unheroic age is dissipated
by the vivid realism with which he depicts the horrors of war.

The reader of the pastoral eclogues of 1606 and 1619 or
of the sonnets collected in 1619 has little difficulty in distinguishing the new work from the old work revised from
the eclogues of 1593 and the sonnets of 1594. We should do
wrong to attribute the change in the sonnets from the
incantatory to the speaking voice ('Shake hands for ever,
cancel all our vows') entirely to contemporary influence;
Drayton could have learnt a lesson from Sidney. Moreover, the change was inevitable as mature experience
forced him to abandon the 'whining' adoration of the early
sonnets. In the sonnet which begins

> How many paltry, foolish, painted things
> That now in coaches trouble every street
> Shall be forgotten, whom no poet sings,
> Ere they be well wrapp'd in their winding-sheet?

the complexity of mood includes scorn and worship, realism and idealism, homely allusion and bold magnificence of phrasing and cadence:

> And Queens hereafter shall be glad to live
> Upon the alms of thy superfluous praise.

Similarly, in the later eclogues there is a blend of idealism and realism, of platonism and of 'country quicksilver'. He does not forget that shepherds still feed their flocks on Cotswold, or that Anker and Stour, rivers of Warwickshire, are better than all the waters of Sicily.

The veil of pastoral allegory barely conceals the poet's contempt for a King and Court who consistently neglected him and his verses:

> The Groves, the Mountains, and the pleasant Heath,
> That wonted were with Roundelays to ring,
> Are blasted now with the cold Northern breath,
> That not a Shepherd takes delight to sing.

In his first satire, the obscure *Owl* of 1604, and in many a later passage, he turns his eyes, too, to the social scene, to the luxury of the Court, the unscrupulousness of gripple (grasping) merchants, and the darker moral vices. But his eyes are not turned so constantly to contemporary society as are Jonson's, nor is his analysis so shrewd and knowledgeable. To him the worst thing about 'this most beastly Iron age' was its neglect of poetry—of that kind of poetry, virtue's handmaid, which might restore glory and splendour to a dull and barbarous land. In the sixth eclogue of 1606 the praise of Sidney is a pointed attack on contemporary poetry. He was surrounded by a circle of friends who held some of the same ideals for poetry—George Sandys, Sir John and Francis Beaumont, Wither, William Browne, the Scottish poets Alexander and Drummond—but those sealed of the tribe of Michael are not so many or so mighty as those sealed of the tribe of Ben. Jonson could feel that on the whole poetry was going his way; but what to Jonson was the sun of royal favour was to Drayton frosty Boreas. In one respect Drayton was like Jonson: he was superbly confident of the merits of his work and untroubled by the doubts or introspection of the age into which he survived.

In what seemed to him an iron age he wrote his most golden poetry; in a time that seemed ignoble and unheroic he sought nobility and heroism. I do not know any lines more likely to appeal to him than Spenser's

> The noble heart that harbours virtuous thought
> And is with child of glorious great intent
> Can never rest, until it forth have brought
> Th'eternal brood of glory excellent.

Drayton has little of Spenser's power of making moral ideas poetical, and the 'abstracted sublimities' of the 'Mutability' cantos were quite beyond him. His simpler ideal is expressed more simply, and partly through heroic action:

> O when shall English men
> With such acts fill a pen,
> Or England breed again
> Such a King Harry?

It is characteristic of him to praise the 'brave Heroic minds' of the voyagers to Virginia and ignore the commercial venture. Poetry, he continued to believe, represents things better than they are; nor is this view incompatible with his attacks upon things that are worse than they ought to be. The kind of poetry he cared for was that

> Which casting life in a more purer mould
> Preserves that life to immortality,

'translunary' poetry in the word he appears to have coined to attach to Marlowe, poetry which casts beyond the moon, which in the greatness of mind that it reveals lifts men out of this earthly mire and links them with gods.

As the present became more and more distasteful to him, he took more and more pains 'to search into ancient and noble things', and a natural inclination to love antiquities, and especially those of his native land, inspires all the poetry and all the prose of *Poly-Olbion*. To be rich in the antiquities of England, like John Stow, was good; to be able to immortalize the natural pieties in verse was better. Beside Drayton's the poetry of Donne or Jonson appears urban; nor is there any poet of his day who displays a more intimate knowledge of the country unless it be his great contemporary from the other side of Warwickshire. There is nothing mystical in his love of nature, but he sought and found in her a pure and durable beauty, and the 'idea' of nature as a perennial reality he found especially in her rivers. 'The gripple wretch' may indeed cut down the forest of Arden, but to this day the 'lively-tripping Rea' flows to the sea through Tame and Trent.

His last volumes of verse were published in the reign of Charles when the poet was in his sixties. They include *Nimphidia*, a poem which, as one of Drayton's best editors has said, 'has the air of a sportive accident' in his poetical development. The fairy world which he invents has clear determinate edges, as sharp and clear as the world of Lilliput; but Drayton's world exists for its own sake. As in Shakespeare, the terror has gone out of the fairies. They are figures of fun to Drayton as much as the devil to Burns in 'Tam o' Shanter'. But they are not 'dainty' like the fairies of Herrick, for there is a robustness in his verses which distinguishes them from the elegant folk-lore of his young contemporary. Above all, these last volumes contain 'The Muses' Elysium' and its precursor 'The Quest of Cynthia'. In the poetry of his youth Drayton identifies his ideal with a Golden Age; in middle age he tends more and more to identify it with the brave old world of the Elizabethans; and in old age he makes an elysium of his own. It is not localized like the earlier pastorals; his shepherds and shepherdesses belong to an ideal world on a transfigured earth. Mutterings from an ignoble world outside enhance the bliss 'gravely merry' of this paradise of poets.

> There in perpetual summer's shade
> Apollo's prophets sit
> Among the flowers that never fade
> And flourish like their wit; . . .

> The Poet's Paradise this is,
> To which but few can come;
> The Muses' only bower of bliss,
> Their dear Elysium.

Perhaps the best description of the luminous style of these last poems may be found in a poem addressed by his admired friend Sir John Beaumont to his despised enemy King James:

> Pure phrase, fit epithets, a sober care
> Of metaphors, descriptions clear, yet rare,
> Similitudes contracted smooth and round,
> Not vext by learning, but with Nature crown'd: . . .
> A noble subject which the mind may lift
> To easy use of that peculiar gift
> Which poets in their raptures hold most dear
> When actions by the lively sound appear.

V

DRAMA

TO explain why English drama should have become great in the years just before and just after the close of the sixteenth century, great as never before or since, to analyse the conditions which made the soil favourable for the genius of Marlowe and Shakespeare, Jonson, Webster and Middleton, is no doubt beyond the capacity of man. Yet without any pretensions to explain what is inexplicable, let me say something, before turning to the dramatists themselves, of the theatre and audience which made their art possible.

If we survey the history of the London companies over the fifty years from about 1590 to the closing of the theatres in 1642, we shall be struck by their development in organization, in wealth, and in importance. This is particularly true of that company in which Shakespeare was the most distinguished shareholder, for it far excelled any other in the quality of its repertory, in the excellence of its acting, and in the stability of its membership. When the period begins, the company has no fixed abode; it acts now at the Theatre, now at the Curtain, now at one of the large London inns. Long before the period ends, it has acquired two theatres, and its takings at the private theatre of the Blackfriars, nearer to the Court at Westminster, had risen to perhaps twice those at the Globe. The theatre had become really fashionable, a profitable investment, the resort of 'silks and plush and all the wits'. Moreover, the fees received by the company for plays acted at Court, or for private performances ordered by the aristocracy and by wealthy citizens to entertain their guests, added more and more substantially to the company's income. As the links between Court and Parliament grew weaker, those between the Court and the theatres became stronger. In 1618 it was a matter of some comment that the Treasurer of the Household and two privy counsellors went to see a play even at the private theatre of the Blackfriars. In 1621 the Spanish ambassador Gondomar 'affably and familiarly' went to a common play at the Fortune, a public theatre. And in 1634 Charles's Queen herself visited the Blackfriars to see a play of Massinger's. It is unthinkable that Queen Elizabeth would have attended even at a private theatre: the plays she saw she saw at command performances at Court. Times had indeed changed from the days not so long ago when those 'glorious vagabonds' the actors of the sixteenth century travelled with fardels on their backs seeking permission to act in hall or inn or barn.

The patronage of the Court made the dramatic companies, or some of them, more prosperous, but did it improve the quality of the plays? Some evidence of the taste of the Court is supplied by the surviving lists of plays acted at Court, and it is not without significance that of the twenty plays acted at Court by the King's players between September 1630 and February 1631 only one was Shakespeare's—and that one *A Midsummer Night's Dream*—while ten were Beaumont and Fletcher's. Amusement and entertainment are important and essential to any theatre, but when audiences seek these alone, when the serious aspects of life are excluded, or are touched on superficially to make a mere emotional titillation, the theatre becomes their dope. In that week of October 1630 when the Court saw a performance of Fletcher's outrageous *Custom of the Country* Sir Thomas Roe wrote to Elizabeth of Bohemia that the public theatres had been closed for six months on account of the plague; 'and that makes our statesmen see the good use of them, by the want: for if our heads had been filled with the loves of Pyramus and Thisbe, or the various fortunes of Don Quixote, we should never have cared who had made peace or war, but on the stage. But now every fool is inquiring what the French do in Italy, and what they treat in Germany.' We may not attribute the decadence of early-seventeenth-century drama merely to the influence of the Court, but it was a contributory influence. The effects are more noticeable in Charles's reign than in James's, but they are to be seen already in James's reign, especially in the last decade of it, after the death of Shakespeare.

The drama is at its greatest in those years between about 1590 and 1620 when the actors were neither poverty-stricken vagabonds nor hangers-on at Court, and when the audience was most representative of City, Country, and Court. With such an audience and such actors a drama was possible that was neither coterie art nor sheer vulgarity and rant, but one that was fed by a wide range of interests. Nor is the necessity of interesting the less educated or rather the less intelligent section of the audience entirely to be deplored. The common people, says Puttenham, have their ears so attentive to the matter and their eyes to the shows of the stage that they take little heed to the cunning of the rhyme and are as well satisfied with what is gross as with what is fine and delicate. But insistence on the shows of the stage, while it may have led to an excessive use of the quaking custard, the rolled bullet, or the tempestuous drum, saved the drama from becoming academic, and attentiveness to matter saved the drama from those over-refinements of style which are the curse of much Eliza-bethan and some Jacobean writing. I hesitate to disturb the ghost of Ben Jonson by hinting that the groundlings may have taught him something, yet their insistence on action did no harm if it turned him from *Cynthia's Revels* and

The Poetaster, both performed at the private theatres, to
Volpone and *The Alchemist*, both acted at the Globe.
Matter he was always ready to give them, and matter they
were always ready to receive, but only if diluted with action.
Moreover, as Sir John Harington and many before him
said about narrative poetry, it is possible with one kind of
meat and one dish to feed divers tastes. Some will feed on
the pleasantness of the story, those with stronger stomachs
will take a further taste of the moral sense, and 'a third
sort, more high conceited than they, will digest the allegory'. *Mutatis mutandis*, this will do to suggest the different
levels at which Shakespeare's plays have appealed from
his day to ours. Even at the lowest level his audience was
sensitive enough to the use of language and rhythm to
listen even when they did not understand. Drayton writes
of the poet's power

> The thick-brain'd audience lively to awake,
> 'Till with shrill claps the theatre do shake.

But it is Dekker who gives us the best contemporary account
of the effect of poetic drama upon the people. He is writing
for the Red Bull Theatre in Clerkenwell, near which he
lived, and for a much ruder audience than that of the
Globe.

> Give me that man,
> Who when the plague of an impostum'd brains
> (Breaking out) infects a theatre and hotly reigns,
> Killing the hearers' hearts, that the vast rooms
> Stand empty, like so many dead men's tombs,
> Can call the banish'd auditor home, and tie
> His ear with golden chains to his melody:
> Can draw with adamantine pen even creatures
> Forg'd out of th' hammer on tip-toe to reach up,
> And from rare silence clap their brawny hands,
> T'applaud what their charm'd soul scarce understands.

We should, however, be misjudging the audience at the Globe if we supposed that it was ignorant and stupid. Webster observed in the preface to *The White Devil* that most of the audience at the Red Bull resembled ignorant asses, but he implies that at another playhouse a dramatist might find 'a full and understanding auditory'. The actor Betterton, when an old man and when the English stage had been ruined, as he maintained, 'by prodigal subscriptions for squeaking Italians and capering monsieurs', is reported to have looked back with regret to the early days of the drama when London supported five or six playhouses and when 'the lower sort of people' frequented the theatre, discovering 'a natural simplicity and good taste when they were pleas'd and diverted with a drama so naked and unassisted by any foreign advantage'. The wealth of sermons and moral treatises available to the dramatists was available also to their audience. The sermon was the most popular form of literature of the day. Without an audience interested in serious matters tragedy is not possible. This audience at the Globe did not wholly consist of groundlings, the 'gentlemen of understanding' who were only so called because they stood under the stage. We hear so much of these because they gave the dramatists most trouble, and next to them we hear most of the foolish gulls who sat upon the stage to see and to be seen. At theatres like the Red Bull these had their way, and especially at holidays, when 'base mechanical men' were at leisure, but at the Globe there were courtiers as well, university men, Inns of Court men, gentlemen and their wives (many of them up from the country), merchants and their wives, captains and soldiers, as well as journeymen and apprentices. I will not lay stress upon Thomas Wright's view, announced in the year of the second quarto of *Hamlet*, that cities sharpen men's wits, and 'this we may

daily perceive in our own country, wherein our Northern
and Welshmen, when they come to London, are very
simple, and unwary, but afterwards, by conversing a
while, and by the experience of other men's behaviours,
they become wonderful wise and judicious', for I know that
this view would be repudiated in Wales and in the North
of England. Nor will I insist upon the view of Thomas
Wilson, a Lincolnshire man, that 'it is much better to be
born . . . in London than in Lincoln. For that both the air
is better, the people more civil, and the wealth much
greater, and the men for the most part more wise.' But it is
indisputable that London being the seat of government and
of the law and (except for the few books published by the
two universities) the only publishing centre in England
was the focus of the nation's intellectual as well as of
its commercial life. Foreign visitors were impressed and
native Puritans shocked by the handsomeness of its theatres
and the splendour of the actors' costumes. When the
Venetian Busino visited the theatre in 1617 he admired the
sumptuous dresses of the actors, the interludes of music,
dancing and singing, the nobility dressed like so many
princes listening as silently and soberly as possible to the
play, and the honourable and handsome ladies. It was of
the Globe theatre that the chief comic actor of Shakespeare's company, Robert Armin, was speaking when in
1608 he dedicated his *Nest of Ninnies* to 'the generous Gentlemen of Oxenford, Cambridge, and the Inns of Court' from
whom (he says) the glories and the livings of the actors
rise and with whom he claims to have seen the stars at
midnight.

One section of society, and one which was becoming
increasingly powerful, never went to the theatre and did its
best to suppress it. Between the theatre and those who refused to grant the moral value of the representation upon the

stage of human vices, who believed that the whole business of this life was to accustom ourselves to despise it and to meditate upon the life to come, there could be no compromise. Philip Stubbes attempted a compromise in the preface to the first edition of his *Anatomy of Abuses* when he allowed that honest and chaste plays might become 'very tolerable exercises' if they were used for the avoiding of that which is evil, and learning that which is good, if they contained 'matter of doctrine, erudition, good example, and wholesome instruction', but he withdrew this concession after the first edition, and there remained nothing to mitigate his statement that playgoers who frequented the public theatres were incurring the danger of eternal damnation except they repent. The Puritans, whether they remained in the Church of England or broke from it, supported their views by quoting many of the passages in which the Fathers had attacked the enormities of the pagan theatres and by more modern instances: the collapse of the floor of a chamber at Risley in Bedfordshire in 1607 when many were killed who had crowded to see a play on the Sabbath day, and the awful case of the young lady who, being accustomed in health to see a play a day, on her death-bed continued ever crying 'Oh Hieronimo, Hieronimo, methinks I see thee, brave Hieronimo' and 'fixing her eyes, intentively, as if she had seen Hieronimo acted, sending out a deep sigh, she suddenly died'. Puritan preachers not only attacked the theatre with *exempla* but with the syllogistic reasoning of which they were so fond: 'the cause of plagues is sin, if you look to it well: and the cause of sin are plays: therefore the cause of plagues are plays'. These preachers were honourable men, and they have left a name behind them that their praises might be reported, but those who believe that the good life is as implicit in the plays of Shakespeare as in the sermons of Perkins cannot but be thankful that London was not Geneva. The City magistrates also would have suppressed the theatres, not only for moral reasons, but for reasons of public order and public health, and because many a tradesman and worker idled away an afternoon at the theatre; and no public theatres were built on ground that came under the jurisdiction of the City. If the stage had not been protected by the Court and the Privy Council, there might have been no Elizabethan drama and no Shakespeare, only a surreptitious hole-and-corner affair such as managed to survive between 1642 and the Restoration.

It has been suggested that Elizabethan drama might have been given 'a larger scope and higher purpose' if it had been taken under the wing of that section of the Church which was prepared to allow to the natural life a richer 'freedom of movement' than that which the Puritans were prepared to allow it. The only official contact between Church and stage was in a censor's office. Plays intended for publication were licensed by ecclesiastical licensers until 1607; after that year almost all plays were licensed for publication by the Revels Office, which had always exercised the right to license plays for performance. Bacon, observing that in ancient times plays were used as a means of educating men's minds to virtue, whereas in modern states play-acting was esteemed but as a toy, regretted that the discipline of the stage in his time had been plainly neglected. But who was to exercise this discipline, he did not say. Perhaps it is as well that Elizabethan dramatists had only to do with a censorship that permitted a reasonable amount of freedom to the human mind. It curbed political and religious speculation of an unorthodox kind, but exercised no such restrictive influence over morals as the unofficial censorship of public opinion over the Victorian novelists.

If we wished to state the prevailing kinds of drama in the early fifteen-nineties with the precision of a Polonius, we should have to speak of pastoral-comical, historical-comical, tragical-historical, and even tragical-comical-historical-pastoral, but in less precise terms we may speak of the chronicle-history play, romantic comedy, and romantic tragedy. And if we ask what the prevailing kinds of drama are ten years later, we shall find that while romantic comedy and romantic tragedy persist, but with striking differences, there is a vogue for satirical comedy or 'comical satire', and that the play whose theme is based on some episode in English history has almost disappeared. It has often been observed that the flourishing time of the chronicle-history play was for a few years before and after the Armada, and contemporary writers like Nashe and Heywood applaud this type of play on grounds of patriotism and morality: 'they shew the ill success of treason, the fall of hasty climbers, the wretched end of usurpers, the misery of civil dissension.' The moral was enforced in poetry, too, in such collections as *The Mirror for Magistrates* and in Daniel's *Civil Wars*. In the preface to the 1609 edition of the *Civil Wars* Daniel observes that his argument 'was long since undertaken (in a time which was not so well secur'd of the future, as God be blessed now it is) with a purpose, to shew the deformities of Civil Dissension and the miserable events of Rebellions, Conspiracies, and bloody Revengements . . . thereby to make the blessings of Peace, and the happiness of an established Government (in a direct line) the better to appear'. Clearly, the need for such a moral was not so great in 1609 as in 1595, yet we should go wrong if we supposed that the history play ceased to be important because of the peaceful accession of the Stuart dynasty in 1603. As I have said, epochs of literature do not wait upon the deaths of kings and queens, and two or three years before the death of the Queen it had become apparent that the vein of the history play was exhausted.

About this very time we notice a change in the temper of comedy. Henslowe's Diary is an excellent barometer to popular taste in the latter years of Elizabeth's reign. From 1592 to 1597 the titles suggest romantic comedies and tragedies and above all chronicle-history plays, but about the end of 1597 it is clear that domestic comedy is becoming popular. We notice under 1598 William Haughton's *A Woman will have her Will* or *Englishmen for my Money*, perhaps the earliest comedy now extant of which the scene is laid in London, and soon afterwards Porter's *Two Angry Women of Abingdon*, and Dekker's *Shoemaker's Holiday*. To this time also belongs Shakespeare's only English middle-class comedy, *The Merry Wives of Windsor*. At first these comedies of contemporary life are either comedies of intrigue like Haughton's and Shakespeare's or are more romantic than satirical like Porter's and Dekker's. Comedy has not here become satirical. Earlier in this decade the attempt had been made to acclimatize the Latin satire after the manner especially of Juvenal and Persius and the satirical epigram after Martial, and in the popular pamphlets of Nashe and others social types and social abuses had been attacked with great force. The drama, however, had remained on the whole untouched by this satirical force, but now at the turn of the century the drama too became satirical, and more and more comedies appeared which were not romantic but were in Marston's definition of comedy 'a spectacle of life and public manners'.

I cannot believe that it was the edicts of 1599 and 1600 calling in many satires and epigrams and ordering no more to be printed which caused this strong satirical movement in poetry and prose of the early nineties to spill over into the drama, for there were signs that the change was happening before 1599. Moreover, the way was prepared for satirical comedy by the new developments which had already become apparent in poetry and in prose; in poetry, the shaking free from many of the more formal figures of sound and the approximation of verse to the rhythms and diction of speech, accompanied sometimes, but not always, by a sceptical critical anti-romantic spirit, and in prose the anti-Ciceronian movement with its insistence on matter and succinctness. We may notice also that in the critical examination of such social types as the gull and malcontent the poets and pamphleteers were before the dramatists. In such a pamphlet as Lodge's *Wit's Misery* of 1596, social satire increasingly takes the form of characters of social types, and the influence of Theophrastus is noticeable for perhaps the first time.

Two years later, and as some say not without some indebtedness to Theophrastus, a great satirical dramatist started on the career which was to leave its mark on English comedy for generations to come. In the first version of *Every Man in his Humour*, acted at the Globe in 1598, Jonson has not quite got rid of eloquence. I do not mean such eloquence as the raptures of Volpone and Sir Epicure Mammon—Marlowesque in their style, though raptures of earth not of 'air and fire'—for these are dramatic, but I mean the undramatic eloquence of the praise of poetry which is spoken by Lorenzo Junior. Such inconsistency of tone is never again found in Jonson, and when he came to revise his first humour play he cut the passage out. In his next play *Every Man out of his Humour* of 1599 he laid down the principles of the comedy of humours. Comedy was to be familiarly allied to the times in theme, in characters, and in language, and it was to serve for the correction of manners. It was, in short, to become what all the theorists of the Renaissance had said comedy ought to be, and what no English writer had yet made it on the popular stage. England has never produced an artist and moralist more consistent than Jonson. From *Every Man in his Humour* until 1632, when in *The Magnetic Lady* he closed the circle of his humours, he anatomized the time's deformity 'With constant courage and contempt of fear'.

'As for laughter', wrote William Perkins, rather grudgingly, 'it may be used.' The laughter of Jonson is rarely laughter for its own sake, and it is never sympathetic laughter. It is usually laughter mixed with contempt or disapprobation. He never spends much pains upon a character that is not either a fool or a rogue. His comedy is a kind of comedy of manners, but a comedy where the manners are not perfect freedom but an object lesson in what to avoid. Etherege reports his society and makes patterns out of it and is amused to do so. He is himself a part of the society he reports. It is his Zion, and he is at ease in it. But Jonson is as uneasy and contemptuous in the society he satirizes as is Pope among his dunces. In his early comedies he seems often to be wasting his powers upon unworthy material. In his later comedies, while his themes are often of the utmost importance to man's life in society, his power of finding an adequate representation of them in dramatic form is dwindling. In his middle plays, from *Volpone* to *Bartholomew Fair*, there is a splendid equilibrium of matter and means, and while his plays are crammed with topical allusions to the London of his day—so that it is to him, not to Shakespeare, that we look for information about Jacobean London—yet their foundations are permanent and indestructible, based as they are on the rascality and credulity of human nature.

His plays are as 'moral' as the old moralities. The difference is, as he hints in *The Staple of News*, that the Vice no longer enters on the stage with a wooden dagger, but as the Vices male and female, 'attir'd like men and women o' the time. . . . Prodigality like a young heir, and his Mistress Money . . . prank't up like a prime Lady'. Vanity, blind zeal, hypocrisy, greed, stupid ignorance, these are among his constant targets. He is, if you like, intellectually arrogant, and he has a fundamental contempt for what he calls 'the green and soggy multitude'. But it is no foolish snobbery that inspires this attitude; for the fashionable gallant, spendthrift and profligate, was to him as much a caterpillar of the commonwealth as the rogues and vagabonds of the lower classes. As he grew older, the changing structure of society brought more and more into prominence the adventurers who in their greed for money and social advancement acted without moral scruple and at the expense of their fellow members of the state. Usurers, monopolists, profiteers, are always attacked by the dramatists. They inherited the attitude of the Medieval Church to usury, and the selfish exploitation of wealth which they attacked upon the stage Lancelot Andrewes and others were at the same time attacking in the pulpit. Of all the dramatists, however, Jonson attacked the unscrupulous greed for money with most force and persistence, most powerfully enforced the view that wealth and rank have obligations and responsibilities. No other seventeenth-century dramatist approached him in this respect save Massinger in *A New Way to pay Old Debts* and *The City Madam*. Jonson's attack is not blunted by sentiment and dilation, as is Dekker's. (Jonson's quarrel with Dekker was in great part the quarrel of an artist: for Dekker was 'a fellow of a good prodigal tongue'.) The weight of his 'strict and succinct style', of what Edmund Bolton calls his 'vital, judicious, and most practicable language', the integrity of his art with its firm sense of relevance, the tough persistence of the man, make his blows effective. As he gets older, his art deteriorates, but his view of life and of society does not change. He is *fortis, et in se ipso totus, teres atque rotundus*.

Romantic drama persists, I have said, into the Jacobean age but with a difference, and the difference between the Elizabethan plays of Greene or Peele and the Jacobean plays of Beaumont and Fletcher is so great that it seems remarkable that they are separated by less than twenty years. Bacon wrote to his *alter ego* Tobie Matthew that it was both King James's and Buckingham's nature 'to love to do things unexpected'; James and Buckingham found the plays of Beaumont and Fletcher to their liking. These dramatists, and after them Massinger and Shirley, are adepts at springing surprises upon the audience. Jonson had done it in *The Silent Woman*, but these later dramatists make a habit of it. A casual clue is often provided in the first act such as

> Were the child living now ye lost at sea
> Among the Genoway galleys, what a happiness!

—a clue which the practised playgoer or reader of these later dramatists would no doubt be able to interpret with some of the satisfaction felt by the solver of a problem in a detective novel. The aim is to stimulate suspense, to give a fresh and unexpected impetus to the plot, or to provide a solution to what appears to be an insoluble tangle. We contrast the method of Shakespeare who gives us all motives, all clues, 'not surprise but expectation' as Coleridge said, and then the satisfaction of perfect knowledge. The sudden surprises of Jacobean and Caroline drama are sought after by men who lay most stress upon plot and narrative. They have a transient effect. In *Headlong Hall* Mr. Gall distinguishes between the picturesque and the beautiful in landscape gardening and adds to them a third character—unexpectedness. 'Pray, sir,' said Mr. Milestone, 'by what name do you distinguish this character, when a person walks round the grounds for a second time?'

This unexpectedness is found not merely in surprises of plot but in surprises of feeling, surprises which are encouraged by the tragi-comedy which these writers affected. How the thermometer of passion goes up and down in a single scene of Beaumont and Fletcher! In that scene in *The Maid's Tragedy* in which Aspatia dies, the alternations of hope and despair are most exciting. 'She lives', 'She lives not', we keep saying, and as theatre it is most effective. But when we put it beside the end of *King Lear*, or, to be fairer, beside the closing scenes of Chapman's *Bussy D'Ambois* or Tourneur's *Revenger's Tragedy* or Webster's *White Devil*, we realize what a superficial stirring of the emotions this is. It is platform pathos.

These writers have indeed their merits. Fletcher ranks high as an entertainer. The one constant principle underlying his work is the desire to amuse. He writes as if he had not a care or a conviction in the world. With no capacity for tragedy or tragi-comedy he attempts tragic passion only to suit the fashion and taste of his audience. A sceptic in morals, an observer only of the superficies of life, he mirrors faithfully the froth and bubble of the court life of his time. That is his criticism of life in so far as he offers any, and we find it not in more ambitious plays like *Bonduca* or *Valentinian* but in such comedies as *The Chances* or *The Humorous Lieutenant*. And Massinger, whose talent is as saturnine as Fletcher's is mercurial, and whose chief interests are political and social rather than tragic, does his best work not in romantic comedy or tragedy but in those two satirical comedies, *A New Way to Pay Old Debts* and *The City Madam*, which provide the most acute analysis of the abuses of the contemporary social scene to be found outside the plays of Jonson.

Beaumont and Fletcher, Massinger, Shirley held the stage when Marlowe, Tourneur, Webster, Middleton were almost forgotten. I suppose that the late seventeenth and the eighteenth centuries preferred them to their greater contemporaries for much the same reasons that William Archer praised the plays of Massinger: the story was more prominent and better-wrought, the characters clearly marked and fairly consistent, and the style clearer and more lucid. A poet of the late seventeenth century looking for easy expression and smooth composition and detesting a style that according to his standards was 'all metaphor and catachresis' would find less to complain of in Fletcher and Massinger than in Chapman or Webster. Yet this very lucidity is a symptom of superficiality and of the impoverishment of their ideas and their language. Massinger's metaphors, as Mr. T. S. Eliot has observed, are often borrowed, and they are weakened in the borrowing; his stock is limited and he uses them again and again; and they are consciously and often elaborately worked out and used as so much temporary ornament with no imaginative reverberations upon the play as a whole. The gift of thinking in images which is characteristic of the best Jacobean drama is lost, and the speech and rhythms of poetry which enable writers like Chapman and Tourneur and Webster to display serious aspects of life with power and concentration are replaced by oratory and spectacle and incident.

But for a few years—years which take in the turn of the century and the reign of James I—dramatists found the words and phrasing with which to express a tragic vision of good and evil with an insight not rivalled by English dramatists before or since. With much that is ephemeral a few wrote plays that in the analysis of civil and private

behaviour are of permanent value. Marlowe was the Moses
who led the way to the promised land, though he did not
live to enter it. He is the first English poet using drama who
possesses intellectual energy. The Jacobeans thought of
him as a great primitive. They speak of his 'pure elemental
wit,' of his raptures being 'All air and fire, which made his
verses clear'. He was to them what Bacon seemed to be to
the early members of the Royal Society. He forged the
New Instrument which was to change for ever the character
of dramatic verse. The suppleness and flexibility with
which Spenser had transformed the rigidity of mid-sixteenth-century verse began to be made available for the
stage. But Marlowe's verse has pace and resonance. He
held the attention of wit and groundling alike, and was the
first Englishman to make of tragedy a form of art that was
both popular and serious.

Milton might not have thought Marlowe 'a better
teacher than Scotus or Aquinas', yet Marlowe's chief
interest lay in morality. To say that he was more interested
in moral ideas than in dramatic character is to say little, for
it is true of most of these dramatists. John Hoskins says
that 'he that will truly set down a man in a figured story
must first learn truly to set down an humour, a passion, a
virtue, a vice, and therein keeping decent proportion add
but names and knit together the accidents and encounters'.
He is speaking in particular of that figured story, the
Arcadia, but he might as well have been speaking of
the drama. Few dramatists, perhaps only Webster and
Middleton, share some of Shakespeare's power of express-
ing a play's moral intention in and through characters that
can be mistaken for creatures of flesh and blood. And
Shakespeare puzzles at times those critics who have tried
to test him by the conventions of modern naturalistic
drama. Marlowe is thought of as a typical man of the

Renaissance, and the famous words of Tamburlaine have often been taken from their context to serve as an emblem of the Renaissance spirit.

> Nature that fram'd us of four elements
> Warring within our breasts for regiment
> Doth teach us all to have aspiring minds.

But to expect in Marlowe's plays or in Elizabethan or Jacobean drama in general a realistic representation of human character comparable to what is found in some fifteenth- and sixteenth-century paintings is to expect what is not there and seriously to misinterpret what is there. In Marlowe there is a strong infusion of the morality play. Greedy-for-power, Insolence, Greed, Pride, are some of his characters. In Jonson, Marston, and Tourneur, also, the characters are humours or moral qualities, and any convention is considered justifiable if it subserves the moral idea. The significance of the names of Jonson's *dramatis personae*, Voltore, Corbaccio, Corvino, Volpone and the rest, is well-known, but it has not perhaps been noticed that Marston in *The Fawn* and Tourneur in *The Revenger's Tragedy* seem to have searched an Italian dictionary for words descriptive of the moral types they exhibit: *Nimphadoro* defined by Florio in 1598 as 'an effeminate, wanton, milksop, perfumed, ladies-courting courtier', *Dondolo* 'a gull, a fool, a thing to make sport', *Granuffo* (in Florio *Gramuffa*) 'a kind of staring, stately, stalking, puffing look', *Nencio* 'a fool, an idiot, a natural, a dolt, a gull', *Piato* 'squat, cowered down, hidden, close to the ground'. The moral attitudes are patent and rigid from the start. If characters change, the change is sudden, as the balloon of a character's conceit or sin is pricked by love or repentance and explodes with a bang. It is the rarest thing outside Shakespeare to find the gradual modification of character by character or experi-

ence. There remains in Jacobean as in Elizabethan drama
a strong infusion of the morality play.

When Chapman says, then, that 'material instruction,
elegant and sententious excitation to virtue, and deflection
from her contrary' are 'the soul, limbs, and limits of an
authentical tragedy', he is giving an adequate description
of important Jacobean drama. It is not so adequate a description of Shakespeare's plays, for Shakespeare stands far
above his contemporaries in the power of diffusing through
his works a 'soul . . . quite through to make them of a piece'.
By his own principles, principles which were based on
his own perceptions, Dr. Johnson was right to condemn
Shakespeare for not making moral instruction more deliberate. It is never more deliberate than in the tragedies
of the two most learned of Jacobean dramatists, Jonson and
Chapman. For this reason we can be more certain about
their private beliefs than we can about Shakespeare's.
Both are profoundly influenced by the Stoic morality of
Epictetus and Seneca. When through the mouthpiece of
his Stoic character Clermont Chapman praises the stage
and its function in society he does so in the words of
Epictetus. Both writers are as much interested in the
political virtues, in man's duty to the state as subject or
ruler, as in the private virtues, in man's duty to himself;
and both dramatists, and particularly Chapman, suffered
more than any from the restrictions imposed by the censorship upon the treatment of political themes. Jonson in
Sejanus gives us a durable examen of the corruption of
tyrannical power and in *Catiline* an analysis of the career of
a political firebrand; and if we wish to find Chapman at his
greatest, we look to the two plays which were inspired by
the career of Charles Duke of Byron. His most famous lines
are those in which Byron declares his boundless ambition
and contempt of danger, lines which express even more

powerfully than Tamburlaine's the rugged and self-suffi-
cient individualism known to Chapman not only in the
world of contemporary politics but also in the old Greek
and Roman worlds.

> Be free, all worthy spirits,
> And stretch yourselves for greatness and for height,
> Untruss your slaveries; you have height enough
> Beneath this steep heaven to use all your reaches;
> 'Tis too far off to let you, or respect you.
> Give me a spirit that on this life's rough sea
> Loves t'have his sails filled with a lusty wind,
> Even till his sail-yards tremble, his masts crack,
> And his rapt ship run on her side so low
> That she drinks water, and her keel plows air.
> There is no danger to a man that knows
> What life and death is; there's not any law
> Exceeds his knowledge; neither is it lawful
> That he should stoop to any other law.
> He goes before them, and commands them all,
> That to himself is a law rational.

The 'atheist' Byron who believes that love, fame, loyalty
are 'mere politic terms' is defeated by Henry IV, the patriot
king, and while Byron is presented powerfully and sympathetically, it is with Henry that victory remains. Above all,
Chapman identifies himself with the two Stoics Cato and
Clermont, who are contrasted with such passionate heroes as
Byron and Caesar: Clermont, the 'Senecal man', to whom

> Well or ill is equal
> In my acceptance, since I joy in neither
> But go with sway of all the world together

and Cato whose last speech before he kills himself is the
Stoic paradox:

> Just men are only free, the rest are slaves.

That Cato should kill himself to preserve his integrity is in accordance with history and pagan morality; that the Christian Clermont should kill himself and justify his action is indeed a surprising departure from Christian morality. Not more surprising, however, than the imputation to the Stoic Cato of a belief in immortality and what seems very like a Christian heaven, in which

> We shall know each other, and past death
> Retain those forms of knowledge learn'd in life.

It is an unusual synthesis of Stoic and Christian morality with which Chapman presents us in his plays and in his poetry, but the synthesis seems natural to this stern and paradoxical writer, who believed that something of the spirit of Homer was infused in him and continually sings the praises of the 'ancient honour'd Romans'.

Both Chapman and Jonson write for the public theatres, but they make few concessions to popular taste. Jonson's aim was to keep tragedy 'high and aloof', and Chapman while basing his plots mainly on contemporary French history infused into them the spirit of Stoic morality, and preserved in his use of the messenger and the long set-speech some of the technical characteristics of Senecan drama. There is, however, another line of drama, less learned and more popular, though retaining many Senecan traits, which descends from Kyd's *Spanish Tragedy* through *Hamlet* and the revenge plays of Marston to Tourneur and Webster. It is here that some critics have found the finest examples of dramatic poetry outside Shakespeare, while others, repelled by the preoccupation of these dramatists with lust and crime and death, have likened the reading of their plays to a visit to the chamber of horrors in Madame Tussaud's. I will not say with Mr. F. L. Lucas that the only answer to those who say 'But people do not do such things' as are done in the plays of Tourneur and Webster is: 'They did. . . . Read the history of the time', especially the history of Renaissance Italy; I will not argue on these lines, for to do so might suggest that the action in these plays was naturalistic. Perhaps the modern reader has to make certain adjustments: to remember, for example, that that age believed in omens and portents, not tepidly and sporadically, but profoundly, so that the effect of the prodigious storm when Essex left London for Ireland 'with furious flashings, the firmament seeming to open and burn' was such that Florio recorded it in his Italian-English dictionary; to remember that the Jacobeans, as the Elizabethans, inherited from the later Middle Ages a preoccupation with death which seems to us abnormal. Their lives were guarded about with symbols of dissolution; the death's head and the *memento mori* were still in vogue. An illustration may make this clear. When the Duchess of Malfi is to be strangled at the order of her brothers, and the executioners enter with a coffin, cords, and a bell, the bellman is impersonated by Bosola, the half-willing, half-reluctant tool of the brothers:

> I am the common Bellman
> That usually is sent to condemn'd persons
> The night before they suffer.

The reference is to a charity presented in 1605 by a rich citizen of London to the church of St. Sepulchre's hard by the prison of Newgate. Money was given for the making of a speech outside the dungeon of condemned prisoners the night before their execution, and for another speech to be made the next morning, while the cart in which the prisoners made their melancholy progress to Tyburn was stayed for a while by the church wall. The words of both speeches are set out in the gift, as also is the refrain, accompanied by a tolling handbell, *Our Lord Take Mercy*

Upon You All. Documents like these illustrate the gulf in taste between that age and this. It has not been noticed that one of the signatories to this gift is a John Webster, but the name is too common for us to be sure that he is the dramatist. Those who confuse Webster's plays with *The Police News* will say that there could be no more appropriate document for him to sign and no more appropriate church for him to worship in than St. Sepulchre's. Yet let us notice that in his play Webster says nothing to recall the speeches of the charity but gives to bellman Bosola verses which express in universal terms the desire for death after overwhelming suffering.

> Hark now every thing is still.
> The Scritch-Owl, and the whistler shrill
> Call upon our Dame, aloud,
> And bid her quickly don her shroud.
> Much you had of land and rent,
> Your length in clay's now competent.
> A long war disturb'd your mind,
> Here your perfect peace is sign'd.
> Of what is't fools make such vain keeping?
> Sin their conception, their birth, weeping,
> Their life, a general mist of error,
> Their death, a hideous storm of terror.
> Strew your hair with powders sweet:
> Don clean linen, bathe your feet,
> And (the foul fiend more to check)
> A crucifix let bless your neck.
> 'Tis now full tide, 'tween night and day,
> End your groan, and come away.

There is no gulf in feeling between us and this kind of writing, and the gruesome apparatus which Tourneur and Webster find necessary should not come between us and the power of their poetry.

The gift of concentrated speech which is one of the marks

of great dramatic poetry is nowhere greater than in Tourneur and Webster; but the writer who next to Shakespeare
gets the profoundest effects of tragedy with the utmost
plainness of speech is Middleton. Unlike Webster he
keeps to verse for his most cutting irony, and he is not
dependent on curiously chosen adjectives or on conceits as
are Webster and Tourneur. His gift of plain statement is
often spent on the superficies of contemporary manners,
but he does not relinquish this plainness in his greatest
writing. We recognize his quality in such spare stripped
sentences as de Flores'

> Push! you forget yourself;
> A woman dipp'd in blood, and talk of modesty!...
> Can you weep Fate from its determin'd purpose?
> So soon may you weep me.

An anthologist in search of pretty passages would find few
in Middleton. His most decorative poetry appears in
passages of searching irony. The lines in *A Game at Chess*
which are said to have influenced Milton in 'Lycidas' are
spoken by a lustful priest attempting a seduction:

> Upon those lips, the sweet fresh buds of youth,
> The holy dew of prayer lies, like a pearl
> Dropt from the opening eyelids of the morn
> Upon the bashful rose.

And these lines from *Women Beware Women* are spoken by a
man just before he hears of his wife's infidelity:

> Honest wedlock
> Is like a banqueting-house built in a garden,
> On which the spring's chaste flowers take delight
> To cast their modest odours.

Under the flowers of Middleton's speech lurk serpents of
vice and suffering.

Shakespeare founded no school, and his development is

unlike that of any contemporary. Yet in seriousness of purpose, in moral imagination, and in the gift of compression by which a line becomes taut with meaning and the disturbance of the rhythm is as much a work of the imagination as the word and the image, it is these men—Tourneur, Webster, and Middleton—who come nearest to him.

VI

SHAKESPEARE

THE speed with which Shakespeare in one short decade transformed the character of dramatic blank verse is remarkable. Inheriting a medium to which Marlowe had given power and dignity, Shakespeare shook it free from the stiffness which still clung to it, began to flash image upon image, to make new fusions of sound and meaning even out of thoughts that were the commonplaces of his age, and without aiming at any preconceived uniformity of structure brought tragic or comic intention into one totality of design. The new complexity which he gave to blank verse is noticeable in *Love's Labour's Lost*. From the opening scene there is a resonance in the verse, an assured strength of diction and musical phrasing, a boldness of imagery far beyond the powers of Lyly, far beyond, it would seem, the Shakespeare of *The Comedy of Errors*, or *The Two Gentlemen*. No one before in English comedy had spoken with such authority and brilliance. Ideas and images crowd into his verse from reserves that seem inexhaustible. To adapt the words of Holofernes, here is 'a spirit full of forms, figures, shapes, objects, ideas, apprehensions, motions, revolutions . . . the gift is good in those in whom it is acute, and *we* are thankful for it'. This civilized piece of high comedy is of all Shakespeare's comedies that which most nearly approaches the special definition given to comedy by Meredith. It is a play in which 'with volleys of silvery laughter' he examines what is 'affected, pretentious, bombastical, hypocritical, pedantic, fantastically delicate . . . drifting into vanities, congregating in absurdities, planning shortsightedly, plotting dementedly'. One of his special preoccupations in the play is the function of language in society, and while he has not entirely worked himself free from that which is out of proportion and over-blown in language, even in the speeches of Berowne and Rosaline where he is least satirical and we may believe most in sympathy, yet he has become more conscious than Berowne of his own affectations. Perhaps it is not fanciful to take Rosaline's questioning of Berowne's 'sans', and Berowne's admission, 'Yet I have a trick of the old rage', as a landmark in the poet's development, as a sign that he was beginning to grow away from the affectations of language and the addiction to figures of sound—parison, anaphora, and the rest—which had fitted so well into the single-moulded verse of his earlier plays. A comparison of the verse of *Love's Labour's Lost* with that in his early historical plays shows that, in words which W. B. Yeats applied to one of his own poems, Shakespeare has 'begun to loosen rhythm as an escape from rhetoric'.

If my first illustration of the development from the early Shakespeare to the later Shakespeare, or if you like from the Elizabethan Shakespeare to the Jacobean Shakespeare, is taken from that often underrated comedy, *Love's Labour's Lost*, let my second be from *Henry IV*, a play that has never been underrated, though critical discussion has been too much confined to analyses of the character and alleged cowardice of Falstaff. In *King John* and in *Henry IV* Shakespeare departed from the pattern of historical tragedy to which he had adhered in *Richard III* and *Richard II*. The main preoccupations are political and social, not tragic, and these are not directed to one centre or character but are distributed over a wide range of interests and characters. The humour of Faulconbridge and Falstaff is not the incidental humour that is found in the Jack Cade scenes in *Henry VI*, where the effect is momentary and has few or no repercussions on the context; it is fundamental humour which irradiates the serious scenes and provides a powerful

commentary upon them. If, as Coleridge says, the test
of Shakespeare's becoming his characters is the truth
and vivacity with which he describes them and enters
into their feelings, there can be no doubt that in *King
John* he identifies himself with Faulconbridge and in
1 Henry IV with Hotspur and Falstaff. Perhaps when
Shakespeare created Faulconbridge his imagination was
already trembling on the brink of Hotspur and Falstaff.
Mr. Middleton Murry pleasantly supposes that the Bastard
divided, by an imaginative fission, 'into the cynical critic of
honour and its idolator; his bluntness and his bravery into
Harry Percy; his wit and his humour into Jack Falstaff'. The
disinterestedness of Shakespeare's art and the wealth of the
materials upon which it works are well shown by this power
of presenting sympathetically two opposite points of view.

In another sense *Henry IV* offers some foretaste of the
tragedies that are to come. Shakespeare had not been
neglectful of tragedy in his early plays, but the gulf which
separates his Elizabethan histories from his Jacobean
tragedies as works of art makes it seem uncritical to use the
same word 'tragedy' about a *Richard II* and a *King Lear*.
In the catalogue *Titus Andronicus* goes for a tragedy, but not
'in the valued file'. Nor is this gulf accounted for merely
by the enrichment and development of his dramatic art
and the advance in his command over all the resources
of language to express imaginatively in word, rhythm,
phrasing, and figure the growing complexity of his ideas.
This Elizabethan world of his is a simpler world, and its
theme is that announced in *Gorboduc*:

> And thou, O Britain, whilom in renown,
> Whilom in wealth and fame, shalt thus be torn,
> Dismember'd thus, and thus be rent in twain,
> Thus wasted and defac'd, spoil'd and destroy'd.
> These be the fruits your civil wars will bring.

But if the Histories are tragedies of a divided state, the tragedies are tragedies of a divided mind. 'My mind is troubled like a fountain stirr'd; And I myself see not the bottom of it'—these words of Achilles are applicable to most of the heroes of Shakespeare's tragedies. If these distinguishing marks of mature Shakespearian tragedy are present in the History plays, they are not present at the centre but at the circumference. The centre is politically England and morally the evils of civil discord. Yet if a hint of what is to come is to be found in the Histories, it is in the character of Henry IV and his tormented conscience at the 'by-paths and indirect crook'd ways' by which he came to the throne.

> How many thousand of my poorest subjects
> Are at this hour asleep. O Sleep, O gentle Sleep,
> Nature's soft nurse, how have I frighted thee,
> That thou no more wilt weigh my eyelids down,
> And steep my senses in forgetfulness.

The imagery looks forward to that of mature Shakespearian tragedy, and already Shakespeare's power is such that he can make a character come alive by an image or a turn of phrase, or can create scenery or an environment or a way of life in a few words, 'infinite riches in a little room'.

But Henry is not at the centre as are Shakespeare's tragic heroes. He is one of many themes that are juxtaposed and balanced in the two plays that go by his name. And if we are looking for the Jacobean Shakespeare, *Henry V* takes us farther from him, not nearer: it is a simple play beside the complexity of dramatic motive and character of *Henry IV* and the richly figured texture of its verse. But in *Julius Caesar*, also it would appear written in 1599, we find a tragic hero in the character of Brutus the foundations of whose soul are shaken and torn by dissension

within himself as was England during the Wars of the
Roses. Now, when Shakespeare's powers are ripe for
tragedy, he turns from the tragedy of disorder in the state
and from Holinshed to the tragedy of disorder in the soul
and to Plutarch. Here and in the two other Roman plays,
for almost the only time, he was fashioning his plays from
the work of a great writer. Plutarch gave him much, yet
contrasted with the welter of miscellaneous information,
moral precept, small gossip, historical detail which Plutarch
crowds into the disunity of his *Lives* is the unity and coher-
ence with which the dramatic idea that lies in and through
the plays is unfolded. In North's prose a Life is no organic
whole. The value of each part is the value of each part and
it is little more. In Shakespeare the power of the whole is
implicit in each part, and each part is an epitome of the
whole.

> O, wither'd is the garland of the war,
> The soldier's pole is fall'n: young boys and girls
> Are level now with men; the odds is gone,
> And there is nothing left remarkable
> Beneath the visiting moon.

Cleopatra's words might be taken as a touchstone of what
is supreme in poetry, but they are greater yet as part of
the flesh and bone of the play. A poet who can speak so
does not give us the characters of Plutarch or of history.
In Goethe's words he does the people of history the honour
of naming after them his own creations.

But in *Julius Caesar* the pattern of his tragedy is not yet
complete. With Brutus the disorder is not brought about
by evil and wickedness from without. He can say:

> My heart doth joy that yet in all my life
> I found no man but he was true to me,

and no woman, too. Of how many of the later tragic heroes

is this true? In *Hamlet*, in *Othello*, and in the great plays that
follow, Shakespeare's characters are symbols of good and
evil, of love and fidelity and endurance, and of lust and
treachery. There is the Jacobean Shakespeare. These
themes had been announced in a few of the sonnets before
they entered Shakespeare's tragic world, at least if we
accept the view that the sonnets were all written at latest
by 1599. The sonnets are not all poems on love and friend-
ship. Some are profound meditations on life and death, on
'th'expense of spirit in a waste of shame', and the 'rebel
powers' that 'array' the soul. But whereas in the sonnets
these meditations exist side by side, many are made one in
the imaginative fusion of tragedy.

If there is terror and pity, there is also love and admiration. Of only one play, perhaps, is this untrue. *Troilus and
Cressida* is not the cynical expression of a man who denies
all virtues and all moral values. It is not an essay in futility.
But it is a play which sometimes intellectually and sometimes passionately analyses moral values, a play in which
chivalry and love are beaten down by treachery and lust,
a play in which the characters who suffer are not purified
as by fire but foully done to death or tortured or warped by
their suffering. I am aware that the Elizabethans did not
take the same view of the Trojan war that Homer and the
Greeks took. A nation that believed itself to be descended
from Troy took care that the Greek dogs did not get the
best of it, nor was Homer himself immune from the satirical
shafts of the pamphleteers of the fifteen-nineties. In a
pamphlet of 1599 which contains a dedication to the
Countess of Southampton, a sonnet to Mistress Mary
Fitton, and a poem by a dark lady in defence of her own
beauty, Homer is accused of making a dog of Agamemnon,
a kitchen-fellow of Patroclus, a madman of Hector, and of
Achilles a mere brothel humour who preferred a brutish

kind of affection before the love of his country and his own peculiar hate before the general welfare of his followers. But references to contemporary views on the Trojan war or on the story of Troilus and Cressida do not explain the uniqueness of *Troilus and Cressida* among the serious plays of Shakespeare. Nor can I think the suggestion that this is Shakespeare's satirical play, written as a 'comical satire' in the deliberate mood that Jonson wrote his *Every Man Out of his Humour*, entirely satisfactory. It accounts for much no doubt: for the treatment of Helen, for example. 'Was *this* the face that launched a thousand ships?' we exclaim and are meant to exclaim, but with how different an intonation and meaning. But if the play began as a satire intended for the consumption of a private and sophisticated audience, perhaps one of the Inns of Court, it ended by being something very different. There are in the play two potential tragedies—a tragedy of war and a tragedy of love, a tragedy of treachery and a tragedy of lechery. It is a double action which Shakespeare never quite succeeds in reducing into unity, and while this would not disturb us in a chronicle play, or a comical satire, where our feelings are not deeply engaged, here is some disturbance, and the mind lacks an assured resting-place. But it is not so much this disunity which separates *Troilus and Cressida* both from the tragedies of Shakespeare and from what Coleridge calls his 'profound comedies'. Nor is it the unevenness of the composition, and the inequalities of the style, which seem to result sometimes from deliberate experiment. To see the difference we may look to the end: the disillusionment of Troilus, whose nature was 'open' and 'free' like Othello's —like Shakespeare's, too, according to Ben Jonson—a disillusionment to which Thersites plays a vile chorus as he creates man and woman in his own filthy image; the accumulation of sordid villainy by which Achilles contrives

the death of Hector; and finally Troilus's outburst of hate
and determination for revenge. A Shakespearian tragedy
usually ends in quietness, if only the quietness of the grave.
But here is no

> Good night, sweet prince,
> And flights of angels sing thee to thy rest.

Here is no

> Vex not his ghost. O! let him pass; he hates him
> That would upon the rack of this tough world
> Stretch him out longer.

There is no other play of Shakespeare's that ends like it.
'The bonds of heaven are slipp'd, dissolv'd, and loos'd', and
what remains is anger and hope of revenge.

To ask whether the mood of this play corresponds to the
mood through which Shakespeare himself was passing at
the time is to beat the air. We do not know, and if we did
the knowledge might not much illuminate the play. That
Shakespeare had sorrows which were more than mythical
is more than likely. But that these had their effect upon his
work in ways that escaped his analysis as they escape ours
is also likely. Shakespeare above all men had the power of
living through experiences not his own, and now his power
over language matched his insight into the depths of man's
moral being.

Hamlet offers a convenient illustration of the road Shakespeare had travelled in so short a time. I know that to
mention *Hamlet* in one lecture on Shakespeare is to be
foolhardy. A man who set out to read all the books about
Hamlet would have time to read nothing else, not even
Hamlet. But I limit myself to a comment upon the rhetoric
of the play within the play and of Polonius. *The Murder of
Gonzago* with its designed antitheses and end-stopped
verse, its set speeches, its lack of articulation between the

speeches, is a deliberate attempt to recapture an old-fashioned mode, and it is in striking contrast, as it was meant to be, with Shakespeare's new style. More subtle, yet easily grasped by contemporaries who had escaped like Shakespeare from the old formalism, is the humour of Polonius's addiction to an outworn rhetoric. It is one way of emphasizing his dotage. That he had not grown with the times is shown by his fondling of fine phrases ('That's good; "mobled queen" is good'), of antimetabole ("tis true 'tis pity, And pity 'tis 'tis true. A foolish figure'), and of agnomination (in his play upon the word 'tender'), or by the string of *sententiae* in the advice to Laertes, or by the examining of the circumstances by gradation with climax in:

> And he repelled—a short tale to make—
> Fell into a sadness, then into a fast,
> Thence to a watch, thence into a weakness,
> Thence to a lightness, and by this declension,
> Into the madness wherein now he raves,
> And all we mourn for.

And when the exasperated Queen seeks to stay this *copia verborum* she does so in words which represent one aspect of the Jacobean revulsion from the Elizabethans: 'more matter with less art'.

As Shakespeare's art became more 'matterful', the choice of a suitable theme became increasingly important. The unfinished state of *Timon of Athens* may be a confession that he had blundered in choosing this theme for a tragedy; and it is arguable that it is the theme which accounts for the difficulty of interpreting the intention of *Measure for Measure*. Of no other play do modern critics hold such conflicting views. The non-naturalistic temper of Shakespeare's plays admits always an element of the morality play, though this is more disguised with him than with his contemporaries because of his unparalleled gift of creating character. If we put *Measure for Measure* beside a play that is roughly contemporary, *Othello*, we feel that its characters are not so sharply individualized, and may more readily be taken to stand for abstract moral qualities, for ethical standpoints, with the Duke as a presiding if sometimes enigmatical providence.

> He who the sword of heaven will bear
> Should be as holy as severe;
> Pattern in himself to know,
> Grace to stand, and virtue go;
> More nor less to others paying
> Than by self-offences weighing. . . .
> Oh what may man within him hide,
> Though angel on the outward side!

If the Duke remained on this level, there would be no problem for us and little interest. But he does not. And as Providence is worsted by Levity, or pales in human interest beside Lechery, or marries himself to Chastity, we may begin to feel that the drama wavers between a morality play and a profound comedy, or that this master of character and language is finding some difficulty in putting the new wine of searching analysis of motives into the old bottles of conventional story.

Othello, too, is based upon an old story, but no critic has called it a problem play. Its outlines are clearer, its shape more comely, its 'meaning' less abstract, and its hero and heroine known to us intimately, as we never know the Duke and Isabella. The utmost abstraction that we find is that the Powers of Light are at war with the Powers of Darkness, that Darkness triumphs for a time, but is frustrated in the hour of its triumph. In this play Shakespeare first expresses powerfully, as he had hardly done in Claudius or Angelo, a vision of evil. W. B. Yeats said of Shelley that he 'lacked the Vision of Evil, could not conceive of the world as a continual conflict, so, though great poet he certainly was, he was not one of the greatest kind'. Whether this is true of the author of *The Triumph of Life* or not, it is certainly not true of Shakespeare, and he gave indisputable proof of this for the first time in *Othello*.

The setting of *Othello* is narrower, more restricted, more domestic than in the tragedies which follow. It is not distanced in time as they are, and does not possess the great aura of association and dignity of *Julius Caesar*:

When beggars die, there are no comets seen;
The heavens themselves blaze forth the death of princes.

or of *Antony and Cleopatra*:

The death of Antony
Is not a single doom; in the name lay
A moiety of the world.

or of *King Lear*:

A sight most pitiful in the meanest wretch,
Past speaking of in a king!

But what distinguishes *Othello* still more from the tragedies which follow is the absence of that iterative imagery of storm and tempest by which the storm within the soul is echoed and enhanced by storm and disturbance and prodigies in nature, so that not only the mind of man but the whole frame of nature, the macrocosm as well as the microcosm, seem to be convulsed. It is as if the evil that creates disorder in the soul lets loose the powers that 'wait on nature's mischief'. In *Othello* the storm in nature is spent before the storm in Othello's mind breaks out. The later plays offer the most obvious and the most sublime examples of 'some favourite vein of metaphor or allusion' running through each play of Shakespeare, to which Walter Whiter drew attention one hundred and fifty years ago.

The language of these plays surprises us as much by its fine excess as by its simplicity. Othello's magnificent line 'Keep up your bright swords, for the dew will rust them' as much as the blunt Iago's

> Not poppy nor mandragora,
> Nor all the drowsy syrups of the world,
> Shall ever medicine thee to that sweet sleep
> Which thou ow'dst yesterday

show how timid are all the rules about decorum and verisimilitude in character. Here, too, is unexpectedness, but of what a different kind from that we have noticed in Beaumont and Fletcher. Othello and Iago speak the lines, and there is power, there is authority, and there is poetry. Of the last 'dreadful scene' in this play Dr. Johnson said 'It is not to be endured'. But the nobility of spirit and language alleviates the pain and makes it endurable. Never more clearly than in these tragedies is seen the truth of Coleridge's statement that 'the sense of musical delight, with the power of producing it' is as much a gift of the imagination as 'the power of reducing multitude into unity of effect'.

It is this power of bringing great things into a sense of order and of musical delight in phrasing and rhythm that makes bearable to us the spiritual darkness revealed in *Othello* and *King Lear*. Iago, Goneril, Regan, Edmund, these are symbols of that evil. It is not right to ask whether they are credible representations of human beings. They are that, but they are greater than that. In their actions, above all in their words, they express the load of evil that is in these plays. Gluttony and Sloth are not there, but all the other deadly sins, Pride, Lechery, Envy, Wrath, Covetousness.

But the Shakespearian tragedy is as powerful in its expression of good as in its expression of evil. There are no more moving lines than Lear's words to Cordelia as they are taken away to prison:

> Upon such sacrifices, my Cordelia,
> The gods themselves throw incense.

The lines move us not because the image is from religious worship, but because they express in little the quality of human endurance and of love which are released in this play.

No compensatory heaven is offered. Man has only himself and his own power and endurance to fall back on. These are very great, but when they fail only madness or death remains, and death is, if not nescience, escape into the unknown. Power and endurance, these help to give strength to this tragic world. In Shakespeare there is no dichotomy between terror and pity as there is in the sentimental tragedies of the naïve Heywood or the sophisticated Beaumont and Fletcher. In a sixteenth-century jest-book there is a story of a Lear of the middle classes and of his slow degradation. An old man allowed his son and his son's wife and children to live with him. At first he sat at the upper end of the table, then lower and lower, then among the servants, and at last on a couch behind the hall door with an old sackcloth for covering. When he was dead, one of his grandsons said to his father: 'I pray you give me this old sackcloth that was wont to cover my grandfather.' 'What wouldest thou do with it?' said his father. 'Forsooth', said the child, 'it shall serve to cover you when ye be old, like as it did my grandfather.' And the obvious moral is pointed. Not even a Shakespeare could have made a tragedy out of 'unregarded age in corners thrown'. An indulgence in passive suffering and the dilation of it is epidemic in second-rate Jacobean drama. I say 'indulgence', for it is false to suppose that there was no sentimental drama before Colley Cibber and Richard Steele.

Shakespeare's unexampled gift of creating character led many nineteenth-century critics to confine their attention to this aspect of his plays at the expense of the dramatic ideas which lie behind the characters or of the language in which these ideas are given expression. The minor characters appear and disappear at Shakespeare's will. Kent is now strongly individualized, now sinks back from personality into generalized commentary. The Fool is dropped without notice when his function in the main purpose is fulfilled. In *Macbeth* many characters are brought in with no attempt to make them individual: the sergeant, the messenger, the doctor, the waiting-woman, the murderers, the 'Old Man', and we may add Ross, Angus, and Lennox. The core of the play's experience is expressed through Macbeth, and these characters are without personality as much as characters in a morality-play. They act as chorus to 'the swelling act Of the imperial theme'. Nothing, indeed, is more remarkable than Shakespeare's power of subduing all his material to one predominant purpose, so that without exaggeration it has been said that his greatest tragedies may be considered as an extended metaphor. Even the comic characters are brought into a unity. (The clown in *Othello* is the one exception.) They are not introduced for 'comic relief' or to relieve tension by making an audience laugh. If they relieve tension it is by variety rather than laughter. We return for a moment to simple people, a gravedigger, a porter, a countryman, and to the goings on of every day, the feeling for bread and cheese, and when we go back to the high tragic mood we do so with a heightened sense that we are moving in a world fully realized, a world in which the moral values are those of our world, which fulfils *all* the conditions of our world.

These tragedies take the shape they have, not only from the nature of Shakespeare's genius, but from the spirit of the age. Yet it is remarkable how few allusions there are in these tragedies from *Julius Caesar* to *Coriolanus* to events that can or ought to be interpreted topically. Such references as that to the child actors which appears in the good quarto of *Hamlet* are exceptional. Nor is this comparative absence of topical allusion due to a strict sense of historical decorum, as it is in Jonsonian tragedy. Shakespeare is continually interpreting the old Roman world in terms of his own, and in idiom and imagery never hesitates to interpret the remote by the familiar. The description of the triumphal entry of Coriolanus into Rome would do for the entry of King James into London. Ross's description of the state of Scotland exactly describes the state of London during the many plagues which infected the London of Shakespeare's working-life. In this respect, as in so many others, he is writing in and for his time yet for all time.

> It cannot
> Be call'd our mother, but our grave; where nothing
> But who knows nothing, is once seen to smile:
> Where sighs and groans and shrieks that rent the air
> Are made not mark'd; where violent sorrow seems
> A modern ecstasy: the dead man's knell
> Is there scarce ask'd for who, and good men's lives
> Expire before the flowers in their caps,
> Dying or ere they sicken.

Again, in the last two acts of *Timon* there run, side by side with the beast imagery, repeated references to the plague; and when Timon urges Alcibiades to

> Be as a planetary plague, when Jove
> Will o'er some high-vic'd city hang his poison
> In the sick air

he mentions three common causes to which London doctors, astrologers, and preachers attributed this scourge of their City: the evil conjunction of the planets, the

corruption of the air, and God's instrument for the punishment of sin. In a writer like Webster we might suspect a
topical reference, Webster who into the last act of the
Italianate *White Devil* puts clear references to the Artillery
Yard, to the menagerie in the Tower of London, and
to Sir Hugh Myddelton's New River. But *Timon* is no
looking-glass for London. Shakespeare does not im-
poverish his art by localizing it.

Throughout the great tragedies there is condensation,
made possible in part by the powerful use of imagery.
While the plot is conducted and the characters talk, there
is this complex of imagery establishing the ideas which lie
behind plot and character. And without condensation
great tragedy is impossible, as the examples of the Greeks
and Dante teach us. But now in Shakespeare's latest
style—in *Macbeth* and *Antony and Cleopatra* and still more in
the plays that follow—there is yet greater compression,
accompanied by a liberty of syntax and rhythm which in
all other writers we should call licentious and which in
Shakespeare leads often to obscurity. As he shifts rapidly
from metaphor to metaphor, jumbles parts of speech,
omits connecting particles, is harshly elliptical, breaks up
the rhythm with internal pauses and light endings, his
commentators often toil after him in vain in the effort to
follow the sequence of his thought. It is no deliberate cult of
obscurity as in Chapman, but the obscurity of a man who has
long been lord and master of all the resources of language,
rhythm, and image, and now uses them with rapidity.

In the two Roman plays of his last years critics have seen
some slackening of the tragic tension which remains taut
from *Othello* to *Macbeth*. *Antony and Cleopatra* is not excelled
by any play in magnificence of conception and style, but
its effect upon us is different from that of the tragedies
which precede it. Here is something of the looser structure

of the chronicle play; here history in part directs the plot instead of merely subserving it; here are other interests which to some extent divert the full stream of passion from the main current, unlike the 'compulsive course' of *Othello* or *Macbeth* which 'ne'er feels retiring ebb, but keeps due on'. We do not feel that the struggle which alone matters is that within the hero himself, or that Antony is torn to pieces within himself. And the powers of evil and hate let loose in the earlier plays, dreadfully enforced by the recurrent imagery, and supported by the powers of nature, do not appear with the same force. Above all, the character of Cleopatra, while it adds to the splendour and wonder of the play, detracts from its tragic intensity. The whole of the last act is given over to her, and she dies in the grand style. But if we ask which of the emotions of pity and fear, love and admiration are uppermost, we shall say it is that one which is perhaps the least tragic of all. We are lost in admiration of this magnificent spectacle. Her death is so glorious as to be a triumph, and she herself feels it to be a reconciliation, a reunion with Antony. 'Husband, I come.'

Beside the strains and tensions, the themes that are balanced or reconciled in this many-sided play, *Coriolanus* is simple in its lines, as simple as the character of the hero. There is no need of an Iago to incite him to his undoing, though at times it seems as if Shakespeare hesitated about casting Aufidius for such a part. Here the reconciliation comes inside the play, when Coriolanus's eyes 'sweat compassion', and he yields to the entreaty of his wife and child and mother. After the reconciliation his death is felt to be almost accidental and in no sense tragic. The lightening of the tragic atmosphere in these two plays has seemed to many an anticipation of the spirit of his latest comedies. *Coriolanus* especially, Bradley has said, 'marks the transition to his latest works, in which the powers of repentance and forgiveness charm to rest the tempest raised by error and guilt'.

Many attempts have been made to explain the change in his art from tragedy to tragi-comedy: he was bored; he was getting old; he had had a serious illness, a religious conversion; he was spending too much time in Stratford and too little at the Globe. There may be some point in remembering that from about the autumn of 1609 the King's players acquired a winter theatre in the Blackfriars nearer to the Court at Westminster, where it attracted an audience at once more cultivated and more sophisticated than the Globe audience, an audience which might well clamour for new fare, for variety of incident, for the oscillation of feeling which tragi-comedy provides, for a greater love-interest than Shakespeare had provided in his tragedies, an audience accustomed to the growing splendours of Jacobean masque and looking for more and more spectacle of vision and masque, more and more music and dancing. Nor did the public theatre of the Globe remain satisfied with the bare boards of the Elizabethan stage, but did what it could to supply a fuller spectacle. It was this audience and this kind of theatre that Beaumont and Fletcher catered for and captured with their *Philaster*.

Some critics, indeed, have argued that in turning from tragedy to tragi-comedy Shakespeare was influenced by the success of these two young heirs of his art, but to do so they have to argue that *Pericles*—which is almost certainly earlier than *Philaster*—is essentially a different kind of play from *Cymbeline* and *The Winter's Tale* and *The Tempest*. Yet many of the themes and even the images which are to predominate in one or other of the last three plays are first announced in the Shakespearian parts of *Pericles*. As in *The Winter's Tale* there is a reversion to the motives of Greek romance popular in the fifteen-seventies. And with these motives goes a background of sea or mountain or desert. The theme is one of loss and reunion, of misunderstanding and reconciliation after a long passage of years. Marina, Perdita, and Miranda are shown in the dawn of womanhood, heroines quite different from the older self-reliant witty heroines of the comedies. Here, too, there is a kind of reversion to an earlier type of heroine—the type of pure and idealized girlhood which Greene was creating when Shakespeare was beginning to write plays—but the setting in which Shakespeare places them and the overtones of his verse make the resemblance superficial. This innocence of youth is set against the vices of civilization and especially of court life: Marina in the brothel, Perdita bred in the innocence of nature far from the intrigues of her father's court, Guiderius and Arviragus reared in the Welsh mountains, Miranda on her desert island. In *As You Like It* Shakespeare had taken his characters into a romantic forest, but in his treatment of the Duke and his followers there is ironic criticism. Touchstone is the touchstone by which we judge the artificiality of their existence. 'In respect it is in the fields, it pleaseth me well; but in respect it is not in the court, it is tedious.' But Boult, Autolycus, Trinculo, Stephano, these do not serve as touchstones, and the contrast holds good between an innocent life in close contact with nature and the rank pastures of the Court. In smaller ways, too, *Pericles* looks forward to the last plays as the essentially different and inferior art of Beaumont and Fletcher does not. Who does not see the resemblance between Marina's

> I will rob Tellus of her weed
> To strew thy green with flowers; the yellows, blues,
> The purple violets, and marigolds,
> Shall as a carpet hang upon thy grave,
> While summer days do last . . .

and the dirge said by Arviragus over the body of Fidele, or feel that Cerimon is a first sketch of Prospero? If it is a question of influence it seems more likely that Beaumont and Fletcher, young dramatists just beginning to write for the company which Shakespeare's genius had hallowed for almost twenty years, took a leaf out of the master's book and blotted it in the taking. Even supposing that Shakespeare were following in the train of Beaumont and Fletcher, his last plays would be yet another example of his power of transmuting the conventions of contemporary drama and touching them to finer issues. Is there 'soft music' in these plays? It is not the exciting sound of melodrama but the suggestion of a symbolism too deep for words. Is there surprise of a kind unexampled in the other plays? The resurrection of Thaisa or Hermione is not the surprise-packet of Beaumont and Fletcher, not a mere device to stimulate or unravel the plot, but that motive of forgiveness and reconciliation which lies at the heart of the play.

Many critics assume that Shakespeare was losing grip upon his theatre and upon his art. In a sense any change from the high tragedy of a *King Lear* to the tragi-comedy of a *Winter's Tale* or a *Cymbeline* or even to the serenity of a *Tempest* is a falling off. But there is no need to suppose that Shakespeare was losing grip. The art of Jonson remains static, but not of Shakespeare. We can imagine some contemporary admirer reproaching Shakespeare for turning to tragi-comedy and complaining that he did not go on writing tragedies, just as we can imagine an earlier and less intelligent admirer complaining that he did not write another *Henry V* or continue in the vein of *As You Like It* and *Twelfth Night*. The seeds of the last plays are already sown in *Antony and Cleopatra* and *Coriolanus*, and when we consider this pattern of his development we ought not to be surprised to find him refusing to continue in a kind of drama

which he had already carried to perfection and moving on
to an experiment in a new kind.

How far this change was his deliberate choice and how
far it reflects a change of spirit admit only of a wavering
solution. Dowden's picture of the Shakespearian ship
'beaten and storm-tossed, yet entering harbour with sails
full-set, to anchor in peace' may be reconciled with *The
Tempest* but sorts ill with the variety of mood and feeling of
Pericles, *Cymbeline*, and *The Winter's Tale*, as they pass in
quick and exciting transition from the low comedy of an
Autolycus or Cloten through the sentiment and pathos
of a Perdita or a Marina, to the pseudo-tragic grief of a
Pericles, a Leonatus Posthumus, or a Leontes. Yet for all
its lush phrasing Dowden's view of these last plays comes
nearer the truth than Lytton Strachey's. There is a change
in the poet's attitude to time and death as it had been expressed in the sonnets, the problem plays, and the tragedies.
Now he is as much concerned with 'things new born' as
with 'things dying'. An assured Providence is on guard,
not only in *The Tempest* where it watches over the beast-
nature of Caliban, the almost sub-human natures of
Trinculo and Stephano, and the evil plots of Sebastian and
Antonio, but in the other plays too. We perceive in

> Pericles, his queen, and daughter, . . .
> Virtue preserv'd from fell destruction's blast,
> Led on by heaven, and crown'd with joy at last.

The qualities in these plays which have led some critics
to call them myths of immortality escape critical analysis.
Behind the apparently simple statement and rhythm of
Ariel's lyric 'Full fathom five thy father lies' is a lifetime
of reflection upon change and mortality, and we are
tempted to say with Ferdinand:

> This is no mortal business, nor no sound
> That the earth owes.

The reverberations of Shakespeare's latest verse give a sense of timelessness, of a spiritual world beyond place and time, which is new in his art. It is not allegory like the houses with high towers and pinnacles merging into 'castles in the air' of Ibsen's Master Builder, but a spirit deeply set in the woven strands of imagery, and the complexities of syntax and rhythm.

> But what music? . . .
> The music of the spheres. . . . Most heavenly music:
> It nips me unto listening, and thick slumber
> Hangs upon mine eyes; let me rest.

The lines like Prospero's comment on his conjured spirits seem to symbolize the visionary qualities of some passages in these last plays, and to suggest the poet's intuition of the mystery of life and immortality. It is as if he himself had heard 'the music of the spheres' and humanity was beginning to grow dim.

NOTES

(The bold figures at the beginning of each Note refer to pages of the text)

3. Burghley's letter is given in full in *Nugæ Antiquæ*, ed. Henry Harington, 1792 ed., ii. 282–6.

6. On Peacham's debt to Elyot see D. T. Starnes, *Modern Language Review*, xxii (1927), 319–22. On the tradition of learning I have learnt much from the unpublished work of Dr. H. M. McLuhan—'The Place of Thomas Nashe in the Learning of his Time'.

7. The quotation from Dekker is from *Four Birds of Noah's Ark* (1609), sig. L2; those from the *Flores Doctorum* may be found under 'Vita æterna' and 'Gloria æterna'. In my edition of *Four Birds* (1924) I underestimated the extent of Dekker's borrowings from *Flores Doctorum*.

7 ff. On what I have called the tradition of belief much has been written in recent years, especially by American scholars: see, for example, Hardin Craig, *The Enchanted Glass* (1936); A. O. Lovejoy, *The Great Chain of Being* (1936); T. Spencer, *Shakespeare and the Nature of Man* (1942); and E. M. W. Tillyard, *The Elizabethan World Picture* (1943).

9. The quatrain is from Sir John Davies, *Nosce Teipsum* (1599).

9. Cf. F. R. Johnson and S. V. Larkey, 'Thomas Digges, the Copernican System, and the Idea of the Infinity of the Universe in 1576', *The Huntington Library Bulletin*, no. 5, April 1934; and F. R. Johnson, *Astronomical Thought in Renaissance England* (1937).

10–11. *The Anatomy of Melancholy*, 2. 2. 3. 1 and 3. 2. 2. 4. For this book I have read Burton in the second edition of 1624 and except for the quotation on pp. 47–8 do not refer to passages added in later editions. Professor Johnson, op. cit., introduced me to William Barlowe's *Magnetical Advertisements* (1616, sig. B1v, and the attack on Mark Ridley in the issue of 1618, p. 5). The passage in Hakewill is at p. 79 of his *Apology of the Power and Providence of God* (1627).

12. It is fair to Dallington to remember that he wrote his aphorisms for Prince Henry: 'To the aphorisms I have given some farce of illustration, which falls not necessarily in the nature of the conclusion; but this I did of purpose to give them better relish in the dainty palate of a Prince and to draw him on with the variety of his viands' (To the Reader).

13. *Raleigh:* cf. *The History of the World* (1614), p. 1, p. 27 (1. 1. 2. 2), p. 97 (1. 1. 6. 9); E. Edwards, *The Life of Sir Walter Ralegh together with his Letters* (1868), ii. 374.

15–16. *St. Augustine, Of the City of God* (1610), translated by J. Healey with a dedication by Thomas Thorpe, book xx, ch. 2, and book xxii, ch. 24.

18. *epiphonematical.* Abraham Fraunce, *The Arcadian Rhetoric* (1588), sig. F3ᵛ, defines epiphonema as a kind of exclamation when after the discourse is ended we add a short 'acclamation' as a conclusion 'in wondering wise'. Example: *Tantæ molis erat Romanam condere gentem.* For the quotation see Sidney's *Works*, ed. Feuillerat, ii. 237.

18. Burton, 2. 4. 1. 5.

19. Lyly's prologue to *Midas* (1592). The passage is cited by Miss G. D. Willcock and Dr. Alice Walker in their edition of Puttenham's *Art of English Poesy* (1936), p. liii.

21. *Gabriel Harvey's Marginalia*, ed. G. C. Moore Smith (1913), pp. 147 and 149.

21. *Justi Lipsi Politicorum sive Civilis Doctrinæ Libri Sex*, lib. iv, cap. xiii (1589 ed., p. 205); *Six Books of Politics or Civil Doctrine*, tr. William Jones, 1594, p. 114. In his address to the reader, not translated by Jones, Lipsius after praising the ancients adds to his scorn of the moderns the words: 'Nisi quod unius tamen Machiavelli ingenium non contemno, acre, subtile, igneum: et qui utinam Principem suum recta duxisset ad templum illud Virtutis et Honoris! Sed nimis sæpe deflexit, et dum commodi illas semitas intente sequitur, aberravit a regia hac via.'

23–4. On the development of Montaigne's thought see Pierre Villey, *Les sources et l'évolution des essais de Montaigne*, 2 vols. (1908), and Jean Plattard, *État présent des études sur Montaigne* (1935).

24. *Essays.* Cf. also the 'Poetical Essays' of Daniel (1599) and the 'Poetical Essays' by Shakespeare, Jonson, and others appended to Robert Chester's *Love's Martyr* (1601).

25. Sir John Hayward wrote the address to the Reader prefixed to Sir Roger Williams's *The Actions of the Low Countries* (1618). For other examples of early attacks on the Trojan ancestry, whether inspired by the political fight between Parliament and Crown or by the cultural fight between 'moderns' and 'ancients', see R. F. Brinkley, *Arthurian Legend in the Seventeenth Century* (1932); G. Williamson, *Modern Language*

Notes, 1935, pp. 462–3; and R. F. Jones, *Ancients and Moderns* (1936), p. 302.

25. Sir William Cornwallis, *A second part of Essays* (1601), 'Instruments of a Statesman'; Montaigne, ii. x, 'Des Livres'.

27. *The Stationers' Register*, ed. Arber, i. 407; ii. 345 and 348.

27–8. The love-letter is in Tanner MS. 169, fos. 58ᵛ–59ᵛ. The subscription is more in the modern style: 'Yours, yours, yours.' The lover was James Butts, but the letter was written for him on 15 May 1579 by a skilful friend, Stephen Powle. Powle was so pleased with his composition that he entered it in his commonplace-book. Butts began to woo the lady when she was not yet 13 years old, and he married her when she was 14, the age when Frances Walsingham married Sidney and Juliet her Romeo.

28. The letter of Lady Jane Grey to Harding is given by John Foxe in *Acts and Monuments* (i.e. the Book of Martyrs), 1563, p. 920.

29–30. The quotations from Hall's Epistles are from *Epistles, The First Volume* (1608), Decade I, Epistle 1, p. 6; the dedicatory epistle to Prince Henry; and (the 'compass' image) *Epistles, The Second Volume* (1608), Decade IV, Epistle 6, p. 176. The firm of Plantin used devices of a hand emerging from a cloud, and holding a pair of compasses, with the motto '*Labore et Constantia*': copies appeared in English books (R. B. McKerrow, *Printers' and Publishers' Devices*, 1913, nos. 334 and 411). N. W. before Daniel's translation (1585) of Paulus Jovius (*Works*, ed. Grosart, iv. 12) interprets: '*Plantin* beareth a compass in a hand stretched out of the clouds which measureth all, *Constantia et labore.*' For *Labor* and *Constantia* Hall has Charity and Faith measuring 'the true latitude of a Christian heart'; but then he insists, in words very like those which Donne uses of a pair of lovers, on the unity of the two and the perfect circle made by the moving foot.

31. Cornwallis, *A second part of Essays* (1601), 'Of Vanity'.

31. *Professor Croll.* In this lecture I am indebted, as all writers on Jacobean prose must be indebted, to some illuminating essays by Professor Croll, and especially to: ' "Attic Prose" in the Seventeenth Century' (*Studies in Philology*, xviii, 1921, pp. 79–128); 'Attic Prose: Lipsius, Montaigne, Bacon' (*Schelling Anniversary Papers*, 1923, pp. 117–50); 'Muret and the History of "Attic" Prose' (*Publications of the Modern Language Association of America*, xxxix, 1924, pp. 254–309); 'The Baroque Style in Prose' (*Studies in English Philology A Miscellany in Honor of Frederick Klaeber*, 1929, pp. 427–56).

32. *Ascham : The Schoolmaster* (*English Works*, ed. W. A. Wright, 1904, p. 265).

32. *Plutarch and Epictetus.* For evidence that they were read in Latin see F. L. Schoell, *Études sur l'humanisme continental en Angleterre* (1926).

32–3. *Sir Henry Savile.* Cf. *Comes Facundus in Via* (1658), p. 122.

33. Quintilian, *Inst. Orat.* xii. 2. 7.

35. *John Hoskins.* M. W. Wallace in his *Life of Sidney* (1915) first called attention to the *Directions for Speech and Style.* It was first printed by H. H. Hudson in an excellent edition (1935), and is included in L. B. Osborn's *The Life, Letters, and Writings of John Hoskyns* (1937). The passage quoted is at pp. 38–40 in Hudson's edition.

36. *Owen Felltham. Resolves* (3rd ed., 1628, p. 43): 'Of the Worship of Admiration'.

36. I quote from the English translation of the *De Augmentis* by Gilbert Watts, 1640, p. 29. When Bacon says that the 'aculeate' style had become 'nostri temporis auribus . . . accommodatum' I suppose that he is thinking of Tacitus on Seneca (quoted by Savile in the place cited on p. 38 below): 'Fuit illi viro ingenium amœnum, et temporis eius auribus accommodatum.'

37. *Anthony Bacon.* The Address is signed A.B., presumably Anthony Bacon; but both Jonson and Edmund Bolton say that it is by Bacon's friend the Earl of Essex. See the Conversations with Drummond and Bolton's *Hypercritica* (*Critical Essays of the Seventeenth Century*, ed. J. E. Spingarn, i. 115).

40–1. See the article on 'Strong Lines' by G. Williamson in *English Studies*, 1936, xviii. 152–9, for many examples. He is in error in stating that the expression 'strong lines' appeared in the first (1653) edition of *The Compleat Angler*; Walton added it to the third edition of 1661. Williamson's article on 'Senecan Style in the Seventeenth Century' (*Philological Quarterly*, 1936, xv. 321–51) is also valuable.

40. Montaigne, ii. xvii; Cornwallis, *A second part of Essays* (1601), 'Of Essays and Books'.

41–2. *Dekker : Villainies Discovered* (1616), sig. K4^v; *Lanthorn and Candlelight* (1608), ch. x.

42–3. S. Hieron, 1605 ed., p. 193. The passage I have summarized is quoted and attacked as a 'slandering and odious traducing' of the universities in O. Ormerod's *The Picture of a Puritan* (1605), sig. A4^v.

Preachers may be divided into three classes according as (i) they freely admitted quotations from and allusions to the classics; (ii) forbade the use of all human wisdom (e.g. William Perkins); (iii) admitted occasional reference to heathen sayings for the purpose of convincing atheists or shaming those who professed themselves Christians (e.g. Hieron). There was much controversy on this point in the sixteenth and seventeenth centuries. For example, Harington mentions a dispute at Cambridge *c.* 1580 and at Oxford twelve years later (*Nugæ Antiquæ*, i. 178–80); and in *A Directory for the Public Worship of God* (1644) the preacher is ordered to abstain 'from an unprofitable use of unknown tongues, strange phrases, and cadences of sounds and words, sparingly citing sentences of ecclesiastical or other human writers, ancient or modern, be they never so elegant', a doctrine opposed by Dr. Henry Hammond in *A View of the New Directory* (1646).

43. W. Dugdale, *The History of St. Paul's Cathedral* (1658), p. 173.

43. William Barlowe, *The Sermon Preached at Paul's Cross, the tenth day of November* (1606), sigs. A3^v, B2, E1^v. If the sermon Barlowe published is the sermon he preached, we must allow for short notice and also for shock; as he explains in the preface, he himself would have been 'one of the hoisted number'.

44. *omne ignotum pro magnifico.* The view that learned sermons had a dangerous attraction for the ignorant is not uncommon. Hieron (op. cit., p. 194) observes that when preachers prefer the ostentation of their own learning before the edification of God's church, the people are brought 'either into such an amazedness as they think that anything may be made of the scripture, or to such an unsettledness in judgement as that they do rather hunt after variety of teachers for their strange manner of preaching than seek for sound instruction for their own better edifying'. Two examples are cited by W. F. Mitchell, *English Pulpit Oratory from Andrewes to Tillotson* (1932), pp. 106 and 120: the complaint of the parishioners of the notable orientalist Edward Pococke (1604–91), whose learning was the admiration of Europe, that he did not quote Greek and Latin; and the observation of South (in the sermon quoted on p. 46 below) that those who were 'the fondest of high-flown metaphors and allegories, attended and set off with scraps of Greek and Latin', were ignorant and illiterate country people. Compare the modern story (if it be modern) of the old woman who took so much pleasure in the word 'Mesopotamia'. In the theatre, too, it was the 'common people' who delighted in the use of long words as rhymes, the common players who ended verses with such polysyllables as *remuneration, recapitulation* (Puttenham, *Elizabethan Critical Essays*, ed. G. Gregory Smith, ii. 86 and 132). The effects are to be noted in such stage characters as Dogberry and Costard. ('Remuneration! O, that's the Latin word for three-farthings.') Middleton observes that in Elizabethan times, the time of the 'great crop-doublet', huge bombasted plays 'quilted with mighty words to lean purpose' were in fashion; whereas in Jacobean times, the time of spruceness, 'single plots, quaint conceits, lecherous jests' were the vogue (*The Roaring Girl*, 1611, Address to the Play-readers).

44. '*it fareth with sentences . . .*': Andrewes, Sermon preached at Hampton Court, 6 March 1594, on the text 'Remember Lot's Wife'.

45. The verses are from James Bramston's *The Art of Politics in Imitation of Horace's Art of Poetry* (1729), p. 26.

45. *Bishop Felton:* cf. Fuller's *Worthies* (1662), s.v. London.

46. *a sting or aculeus:* Harington in *Nugæ Antiquæ*, ed. cit. i. 168.

46. *South:* sermon preached on 30 April 1668 (*Twelve Sermons and Discourses*, 6th ed., 1727, v. 436).

46. *Dallington: Aphorisms* (1613), To the Reader.

46–7. *Burton.* The quotations are from 'Democritus to the Reader', 3. 1. 3. 3, and 3. 4. 2. 3. The passage on religious melancholy from 3. 4. 2. 3 I quote not from the second (1624) edition but from the fuller version in the third (1628) edition.

49. For Perkins's influence see Perry Miller's *The New England Mind* (1939). His fine study contains the best available account of the influence of Pierre de la Ramée (Petrus Ramus) who provided a short cut to the logic of Aristotle and who gave *inventio, dispositio,* and *memoria* to logic, leaving to rhetoric only *elocutio* and *pronuntiatio.* Harvey and Sidney were Ramists, as were many Puritans. The fact that Ramus was one of the victims of St. Bartholomew's Day—he appears as a character in Marlowe's *Massacre at Paris*—helped to endear him to the Puritans. I have said nothing about his influence because I do not know enough; as Burton says of astronomical speculation, 'I leave the contemplation of these things to stronger wits'. In particular, I do not know how the influence of Ramus on Perkins is to be distinguished from that (say) of Calvin. Mr. Perry Miller writes (p. 327): 'As soon as a minister became indoctrinated with Ramist ideas, he was surely forced by its inescapable tendency to divorce thought from expression, to dissever content from style;

he was committed to working out his sermon structure in terms of logic, and only thereafter going over his work to punctuate it with tropes or to cast sentences into schemes. He certainly could not, for instance, any longer pour out his thought in sinuous word-patterns that echoed and re-echoed the phraseology of his texts, or that coiled around the fervid imagery of the Bible in reiterative incantations.' But while Calvinists were glad to defend their methods by the doctrine of Ramus, their attachment to dialectics rather than rhetoric is too deep-rooted to be attributed to the influence of one man. Sir Herbert Grierson writes: 'For the Protestant, as perhaps for St. Paul, the earthly life of Christ was subsumed and transcended by the great truths of the Eternal Decrees of God and man's salvation through the imputed righteousness of Christ'; and he observes that in his grandmother's Free Kirk house the test of the godliness of wandering ministers was that they read at family prayers from the Epistles of St. Paul, not from the Gospels (*Cross Currents in English Literature of the XVIIth Century*, 1929, p. 99).

49. J. Hall, *Epistles, The First Volume* (1608), Decade I, Epistle 7, p. 72.

49. Perkins's adversary was William Bishop in *A Reformation of a Catholic Deformed: by M. W. Perkins* (1604), cited by J. Bass Mullinger in the *Dictionary of National Biography*.

50. For Perkins's instructions to preachers see *The Art of Prophecying, Works*, 1609, ii. 759.

50. *Swift:* Tatler 230.

51. Walton's report appears to be apocryphal: see the *Dictionary of National Biography*. For the quotations that follow, see *The Times*, 12 February 1943, and Sidney's *Works*, ed. Feuillerat, iii. 124.

51–2. *he durst and knew:* Sidney, ed. cit. i. 42 and 97; Dallington, *The View of France* (1604), sig. S3; Hayward, op. cit., sig. A1^v.

53. *The Faerie Queene*, II. ii. 44. T. Warton, *Observations on the Faerie Queene* (1754), p. 82. Harvey, op. cit., p. 162; see also pp. 160–1 for Harvey's praise of Chaucer's and Lydgate's astronomical learning— 'It is not sufficient for poets to be superficial humanists, but they must be exquisite artists and curious universal scholars'. What was necessary for a poet, however, might be excessive for a gentleman. A gentleman, says Cornwallis (*A second part of Essays*, 1601, 'Of Essays and Books'), needs only as much astronomy as will enable him to see the revolutions of the heavens 'without dismayedness'.

55. *Diary of John Manningham*, ed. J. Bruce, 1868, p. 156; T. Dekker, *A Knight's Conjuring* (1607), sig. B2 (ed. E. F. Rimbault, 1842, p. 9).

56. Harington: *Nugæ Antiquæ*, ed. cit. ii. 211.

57. Brightman : *The Preces Privatae of Lancelot Andrewes*, ed. F. E. Brightman (1903), p. xxx.

58. '*Whose every work . . .*': Jonson, *Epigrams*, 'To John Donne'.

60. Raleigh's contemporary admirer was Henry Buttes, *Diet's Dry Dinner* (1599), sig. P5.

60. Anton : *The Philosopher's Satires* (1616), sig. L4ᵛ.

64. *The Excursion*, iv. 324–31. In a note Wordsworth observes that the last two lines are translated from Seneca. W. Knight gives the reference to *Natur. quaest.*, lib. 1, praef. 4: 'O quam contempta res est homo, nisi supra humana surrexerit.'

65. The verses are from John Chudleigh's elegy on Donne as quoted in Walton's *Life*. I am indebted in this paragraph to L. F. Benson's *The English Hymn* (1915).

67–8. Hall's versions of the Psalms are reprinted in Grosart's edition of the *Complete Poems* (1879), pt. ii, pp. 195–213. He answers his critics in *Epistles, The First Volume* (1608), Decade II, Epistle 5.

69. The quatrain is by John Vicars: *Du Bartas His Divine Weeks and Works*, 1633, sig. A6.

73. *Walsingham*. The poem is printed by Hales and Furnivall in *Bishop Percy's Folio Manuscript*, iii (1868), 470–1, and in L. Guiney's *Recusant Poets*, i (1938), 355–6. For the text of 'Hierusalem, my happy home' see Guiney, i. 269–72 and 278–82.

75. Griffin's borrowings from Southwell are noted by Charles Crawford in his copy of Southwell's *Poetical Works*, ed. W. B. Turnbull, 1856, now in my possession.

84. On the fashionableness of the theatres and the takings at the Blackfriars, see G. E. Bentley, *The Jacobean and Caroline Stage* (1941), i. 30, 42.

85. *Gondomar . . . Charles's Queen.* Cf. John Chamberlain, *Letters*, ed. N. McLure, ii. 181, 391; Bentley, i. 39. The performance at the Blackfriars may have been a private one specially given for the Queen; this was not her only visit.

85. For the performances at Court in 1630–1 see Bentley, i. 27–8.

In 1668, Dryden writes, two of Beaumont and Fletcher's plays were acted for one of Shakespeare's or Jonson's: 'the reason is, because there is a certain gaiety in their comedies, and pathos in their more serious plays, which suits generally with all men's humours' (*Essays*, ed. Ker, i. 81).

85. *Sir Thomas Roe : State Papers Domestic*, Charles I, vol. 174, doc. 102.

87. *Harington: Elizabethan Critical Essays*, ed. G. Gregory Smith, ii. 203.

87. Drayton, *Works*, ed. Hebel, ii. 358; Dekker, Prologue to *If It Be Not Good*.

88. Charles Gildon, *The Life of Mr. Thomas Betterton* (1710), p. 143.

88–9. T. Wright, *The Passions of the Mind* (1604), sig. A4^v; T. Wilson, *The Art of Rhetoric* (1560), ed. G. H. Mair, p. 13.

89. *Busino:* cf. *The Quarterly Review*, vol. 102 (1857), p. 416; and the Calendar of Venetian State Papers, 1617–19, xv. 67.

90. P. Stubbes, *The Anatomy of Abuses* (1583), ed. F. J. Furnivall, I. x and 145.

90. *Modern instances:* T. Beard, *The Theatre of God's Judgements*, 1612 ed., p. 212; R. Brathwait, *The English Gentleman*, 1652 ed., p. 109.

90. *Syllogistic reasoning:* see the sermon by T. W. preached 3 November 1577; cited in F. J. Furnivall's edition of Harrison's *Description of England*, part iv (1908), p. 344.

91. *It has been suggested . . .* Cf. H. J. C. Grierson, *Cross Currents* (1929), pp. 82 and 129.

91. *De Augmentis*, II. xiii.

92. Nashe, ed. McKerrow, i. 213.

94. In style and form Lodge's *Wit's Misery* resembles Nashe's *Pierce Penniless* (1592), in style in its 'Ciceronian' eloquence and in its blend of a high style with racy images and allusions, and in form in its attack upon the seven deadly sins of London, an attack in which in the manner of the time many passages are 'conveyed' from Lodge's reading in florilegia of the Fathers and in other works, while the topical references to London's underworld come from his own extensive knowledge. Lodge, however, is indebted, as Nashe is not, to the Characters of Theophrastus, a work which Casaubon's Latin translation of 1592 had made more available to Europe, although Lodge's characters are not written in the witty pointed style which became characteristic of the hundreds of characters written in the seventeenth century.

> This is a right malcontent devil. You shall always find him his hat without a band, his hose ungartered, his rapier *punto renverso*, his looks suspicious and heavy, his left hand continually on his dagger. If he walk Paul's, he skulks in the back aisles, and of all things loveth no societies. . . . Well spoken he is, and hath some languages, and hath read over the conjuration of Machiavel. In belief he is an Atheist or a counterfeit Catholic, hating his country wherein he was bred, his gracious prince under whom he liveth . . . not for default either in government or policy, but of mere innated and corrupt villainy and vain desire of innovation.

C. R. Baskervill writes of this pamphlet as a precursor of Jonsonian comedy in *English Elements in Jonson's Early Comedy* (1911).

95. W. Perkins, *A Direction for the Government of the Tongue* (*Works*, 1603 ed., p. 533a).

96. Bolton, *Hypercritica*, ed. cit. I. 111.

97. *Bacon to Tobie Matthew:* cited by A. H. Mathew and A. Calthrop, *The Life of Sir Tobie Matthew* (1907), p. 198.

97. '*Were the child living . . .*': *Monsieur Thomas*, I. i.

99. '*all metaphor and catachresis*'. Cf. James Wright, *Country Conversations* (1694), ed. C. Whibley, 1927, pp. 34–5, and Dryden's attack on *Bussy D'Ambois* (*Essays*, ed. Ker, i. 246).

100. Hoskins, ed. cit., p. 41.

101–2. On the rarity of character-development outside Shakespeare see M. C. Bradbrook, *Themes and Conventions of Elizabethan Tragedy* (1935), pp. 61–2. The quotation from *Bussy D'Ambois* on p. 102 (a 'soul . . . quite through . . .') is cited by Miss Bradbrook (p. 96).

102. *When Chapman says . . .:* Dedication to *The Revenge of Bussy D'Ambois*.

105. J. Florio, *Queen Anna's New World of Words* (1611), s.v. *Ecnephia*.

105–6. *Letter Book* CC (Guildhall Record Office, London), fos. 60b to 61b; another copy of this document is in *Journal of the Court of Common Council*, vol. 26, fo. 332. John Webster signed his name as

Common Councillor. I do not believe that there is a reference to Robert Dowe's (or Dove's) gift in Lady Macbeth's

> It was the owl that shriek'd, the fatal bellman,
> Which gives the stern'st good-night.

Here the metaphor is compounded of the owl as a bird of ill omen and the bellman crying his nightly news of time and weather. Cf. *Blurt, Master-Constable* (1602), III. i. 104:

> the owl, whose voice
> Shrieks like the bellman in the lover's ears.

111. *the truth and vivacity . . .:* cf. *Coleridge's Shakespearean Criticism*, ed. T. M. Raysor (1930), ii. 217.

111. J. Middleton Murry, *Shakespeare* (1936), p. 170.

114. *a pamphlet of 1599. A Woman's Worth*, with dedications by A. Gibson. It purports to be translated from the French of 'a Lord of great reckoning' by a friend of Gibson's and fellow-servant to the Queen.

117. On the importance of a suitable theme see J. J. Chapman cited by W. W. Lawrence in *Shakespeare's Problem Comedies* (1931), p. 222; and for an excellent analysis of *Timon of Athens* as an unfinished play see Dr. Una Ellis-Fermor's article in *The Review of English Studies*, xviii (1942), 270–83.

119. On the imagery in *Othello* see G. Wilson Knight, *The Wheel of Fire* (1930), p. 122.

121. *No compensatory heaven:* cf. I. A. Richards, *Principles of Literary Criticism* (1928 ed.), p. 246.

121. *Merry Tales* (1567), no. ciii: reprinted in W. C. Hazlitt's *Shakespeare Jest-Books* (1864).

122. On the part of Kent see H. Granville-Barker, *Prefaces to Shakespeare, First Series* (1927), pp. 195–7.

125. *history in part directs the plot . . .:* cf. *Coleridge's Shakespearean Criticism*, ed. cit. i. 143.

129. *'things new born'*. This passage from *The Winter's Tale*, III. iii. 101, is referred to in a similar context in Theodore Spencer's *Shakespeare and the Nature of Man* (1943 ed.), p. 186.

INDEX OF NAMES